Don Cupitt

The Revelation of Being

SCM PRESS LTD

0 334 02744 6

First published 1998
by SCM Press Ltd
9–17 St Albans Place, London N1 0NX

Typeset at Regent Typesetting, London
and printed in Great Britain by
Biddles Ltd, Guildford and King's Lynn

Contents

Foreword

As will soon become clear, this new essay is a spin-off from the writing of *The Religion of Being* in the spring and summer of 1997. In that book I used Heidegger as a foil in order to appropriate some of his vocabulary, and so induce myself to rethink a number of matters from a new angle. The result was a brief period of high excitement, and a very late-twentieth-century lesson: one should not get stuck for life with a single final vocabulary.[1] It is refreshing, even revitalizing, to change bits of one's own final vocabulary from time to time.

This last point affects both the method of the present book and the way it should be read. As will soon be seen, I introduce three terms of art, Being, Man and Language, each of which is used in a special sense that owes something to Heidegger. I write around them and relate them to each other in a way that is intended to create an effect of revelation and a feeling of religious happiness. And you may wonder what may be the point of proceeding in this way. You may accept that because of the secularization of modern culture, what used to be called 'Theology' is turning into religious writing and becoming simply philosophy of life, or *Lebensphilosophie* as the Germans call it. This relatively novel kind of writing will aim to show what it is to take a religious view of life, and will seek to draw religious meaning and religious happiness out of the middle of ordinary language and everyday life. And all this, you may already agree with; but in that case, why introduce any special technical terms at all? Surely my project requires me to use nothing but the most everyday vocabulary?

I reply that religious writing, like painting, will not work if it merely copies ordinariness. It is necessary to cleanse the doors of perception. My three technical terms are intended to change your angle of vision a little, and thereby to help you to break with the past, and to see ordinariness – just the view out of your window, just the world of everyday human life – in a new way.

It seems then that under today's conditions any philosophy-of-life, or religious, writing will have something of the character of a work of art. It will introduce a few special terms in order first to de-familiarize the everyday, and then to return the reader into it. In the Middle Ages, and even until the late eighteenth century, writing in philosophy and religion could draw upon a standard vocabulary, just as painting followed a standard iconography, and one could assume its general intelligibility. Today, and for all sorts of good reasons, that is no longer the case. The world is more plural, and philosophical and religious writing is more plural. And because there is now no standard vocabulary to draw upon, even somebody as determined to be content with ordinariness as I am is obliged to push meanings around a bit and to play a few tricks, both with language and upon the reader, in order to produce the desired effect.

The first Western religious thinker of real note to be a literary pluralist was Kierkegaard, who has four or five different *personae*, each with his own distinctive style of thinking and final vocabulary. There is the aesthetic writer, the sober moralist, the religious writer and the Christian writer; and Kierkegaard the diarist is perhaps a fifth person who presides over and comments upon the performance of the other four.

It took over a century for people to recognize the extent and the implications of Kierkegaard's originality here.[2] Before his time it had almost always been thought by both theologians and philosophers that there is such a thing as *getting it right*, when one's own final vocabulary and ways of thinking are successfully tracking and transcribing the objective intelligible order of things. There is one Logos, one intelligible order of things out there, and just one true description and history of the world. The universe *itself* has a final vocabulary, laid up in the noumenal world or in the divine Mind. The human thinker's task is to produce a miniature replica in a book or series of books of the objective rational system of things. Western thinkers were mostly pretty confident that in the philosophical tradition that stemmed from Plato, and/or in the theological tradition that stemmed from the Bible and the Christian Fathers, the right final vocabulary could be found. One could *get it right*, and when a thinker had determined his own final vocabulary, and had built and published his system, he truly believed that there was no more to be said. He had stated the Truth, and the Truth does not change. When the human mind is conformed to the Divine Mind, or to the Logos of things out there, one can in principle produce a book that simply gets it right; and if you think like that, it will never occur to you that you might do yourself a favour by changing some of your own keywords and trying out a few new ones.

This classical style, in both philosophy and theology, was 'dogmatic' or 'realistic' – which means that tradition and social authority combined to produce a great effect of objectivity. People believed that the human thinker thought aright and attained to the Truth when his thinking was fully conformed to what philosophy called the objective Order of Reason, or to what religion called the Mind of God. (Amongst theologians, the belief in objective dogmatic Truth was also tied up with the belief that God's Last Word had been spoken, and had been correctly heard by us.)

In the great German Idealist philosophers one can see this tradition remaining influential even as it is coming to an end. Kant, Hegel and Schopenhauer, for example, all eventually produce and identify themselves with systems, and each of them thinks of his own system as final. Each talks as if he thinks he is really finishing philosophy, even while Kant's critical thinking, Hegel's historicism, and Schopenhauer's atheism and pessimism, all foreshadow the end of the dream of an attainable objective systematic Truth of things.

Coming after and reacting against German Idealism, Kierkegaard is literary, a pluralist and the first postmodernist. He rejects the idea of the System (or as we now say, capital-P Philosophy) as being incompatible with our personal experience of time and change and the ambiguities of life. We should give up the idea that there is one objective Truth of everything sitting out there, written presumably in 'mentalese', the universal language of thought, and ready and waiting for us to come along and read it, track it, and transcribe it into a text. Henceforth, human beings are going to have to live with the idea that several different religions, philosophies, forms of consciousness and visions of the world are workable, and none can be proved to be simply and dogmatically True. We are going to have to create and choose our faiths for ourselves. Truth is no longer laid on for us in quite the old way.

These developments bring philosophy and theology very close to imaginative literature. A person who writes a book in either of these fields is producing a work of art and recommending a certain vision of the world. And correspondingly the believer who sets out to live by a religious or a philosophical vision can do so only on the basis that I have in the past described as 'active non-realism'. This doctrine was an updated version of the existentialist appeal to decision and commitment. One just *chooses* to enact in life a certain vision of the world, and to make it come true just by living it.

It follows that all religions, philosophies of life and visions of the world are human imaginative constructions – and none the worse for that. The truth in a religious or philosophical text is no longer seen as corresponding to, or as being isomorphous with, a great Objective Truth out there. There is no Truth out there; the truth is only in the text. Truth is a property of

4

sentences only, so that we are the only makers of truth. And similarly, there is no Meaning out there beyond our language. Meaning depends only on the way words are used, the jobs they do in sentences, and their relations with other words. The meaning is only in the words. Theology and philosophy become not just Arts subjects but *art* subjects, endless in the way that art is endless. We have given up the idea of a final truth. There are no last words. We are trying to invent workable and intellectually-persuasive portrayals of the human situation and the good life; but we are not copying anything. We are just making it all up, out of the available vocabulary.

These considerations bring out the difficulty of a religious writer's task today. The English language, along with most of English life, has been pretty heavily secularized since the later seventeenth century by commercial and technological rationality: that is, by trade and commerce, buying and selling, science and technology. Modern English no longer readily expresses philosophical, or religious, or even ethical ideas. But the language happily remains very rich in idioms and in possibilities for saying more *via* puns, allusions, hidden quotations and so on.

This is to say that in order to insinuate a philosophical point in modern English, you must play tricks, and exploit the available idioms. For example: if in the dusk you strain your eyes, you may be able to *make out* a dog a little way ahead. The idiomatic phrase 'make out' conveys with great elegance and simplicity a philosophical point about perception as a world-building activity, which the average English-speaking person would regard as outrageously paradoxical if you were to put it to him more directly.[3] Our idioms are much cleverer than most of us are, and they are the religious writer's best allies.

In philosophical and religious writing today, I am saying, everything depends upon command of language; upon attention to the fine detail of vocabulary, rhetoric and idiom. When I change some of my key words, or 'final vocabulary', I don't find myself merely trying to say the same old things in new words. I find myself excitedly saying new things and *making out* new truths. A new vocabulary builds a new world.[4]

In the scriptural religious traditions, what is called 'orthodoxy' represents an attempt by the authorities to use law to enforce a fixed and immutable final vocabulary and set of permitted idioms. 'Orthodoxy', for reasons of its own, seeks the end of religious thought and tries to bring about a condition of permanent servitude and religious immobilism. It has been wonderfully successful: we have found that it is perfectly possible for a religious tradition to endure for a thousand years and more with hardly any change. Such a tradition is spiritually sterile; it produces nothing whatever – but it survives, and perhaps that is what many people admire most. Longevity, even the longevity of a living fossil, is considered to be an achievement.

Not today, however. Today, if anything of religion or philosophy is to survive, there has to be linguistic deviation, heresy and experiment. So I am a deviant, somebody who wanders off the right road, and I hope to interest you in deviancy. Fare well.

*   *   *

I hope it will be understood that the word Man is used here to signify the species as a whole (*homo* or *anthropos*, the concrete universal, Humanity), together with the whole world that human beings have built around themselves. No special reference to the male sex is intended. I have simply been unable to find a better term for the human world, the world of human life and experience, the world of *Dasein*, the world of consciousness, the world we know and own; a word which would bring out the force of our modern realization that we haven't been *inserted into* a world ready-made for us, and we haven't been *given* language and consciousness, but rather that we *ourselves* have laboriously evolved all these things. Only we – so far as we can tell – have developed language, thought, and a complex known world about ourselves. We have evolved all these things 'immanently', and, as they say, from scratch.

This is a strange realization, hard to grasp. It makes us think that we must see ourselves, our ordinary language and our life-world as somehow being philosophically primitive, in a way that I seem to need the word 'Man' to convey. I hope its use will not seem any more objectionable or politically-incorrect than the use of the word goose for the whole kind, as well as for one sex. Is anybody seriously worried on behalf of ganders?

Thanks once again to friends who have read and commented on my drafts, and to Linda Allen for typing.

Cambridge, 1998   D.C.

1. Bliss

One day in July 1997 I was sitting at my desk, writing *The Religion of Being*. I was thinking about the perfect mutual fit and the coextensiveness of Being and Language, and their coming together in 'Man' – that is, in *us*, in the human world, in the field of consciousness, in *all this* that is before our eyes. I was looking out of the window across the broad panorama of Parker's Piece, at moving clouds, kites, cars, groups of walkers and cyclists. I saw the whole scene as covered over with and made legible by language; as be-ing, coming continually forth into expression; and as the human world, *my* world. Outside-lessly, the coming-together of Being and Language, not just *in* Man but *as* Man – that is, as the human world: three in one, the worlds of Being, of Meaning, and of human life. These thoughts mounted. An all-round, unobstructed, clear understanding of things, which included me, seemed to dawn. There was an instant like the moment when a tightly-coiled spring begins to release its energy, and then a violent explosion of pure happiness which passed so rapidly that I became conscious of it and identified it only as something that was already fast receding and becoming forgotten. I found myself snatching at it as it slipped away, melting through my fingers.

In the history of philosophy and religion such moments have often been thought of as jumping clear of language and ordinary reality, and offering us a brief glimpse of a higher order of being. The vocabulary that is usually invoked includes words like ecstasy, intuition, insight, enlightenment, nirvana, *satori*,

8

vision, the Vision of God, contemplation, light, salvation, warmth and so on. The metaphors are predominantly visual, implying that with one's mind's eye one enjoys a direct but tantalizingly-brief peep into an invisible intelligible world which may be described as either the noumenal world of Platonism, or the heavenly world of religion. It has always been supposed that even the briefest glance into this Higher World will cause one to feel great happiness. It is felt to be a world of bliss, a world of light. It is felt to be our true home from which we have been exiled, and we take the experience as a promise that one day we will return to it for ever.

I have had such an experience, on average, every few years since early childhood. The first of them were indeed strongly visual. The earliest of all occurred in the summer of 1938 or 1939, when I was four or five years old. I had been taken by my parents to visit a family named S——, and played in their garden with their daughter Rachel, who was of my age. I saw her blonde head against the declining sun, which appeared to set her hair on fire and made her look like a heavenly visitant. I never saw her again, but sixty years afterwards I still remember being suddenly and violently smitten, and even stricken. After that, it would have to be a blonde.

Some other similar events were equally visual. One, involving a very large and old wistaria plant seen in cerulean bloom and bright sunshine, is briefly analysed in *Taking Leave of God* (1980), c.2 (p.30), and is reported there as having taken place in 1955. Another occurred as recently as October 1992, as I came out of intensive care in the neurosurgery unit at Addenbrooke's Hospital. Although in extreme headpain, I saw a glitter of sunlight in the corner of the window of the ward, and was suddenly happy. It was divine, it was the old mythological shower of gold. The metaphor of the sun and 'solar' spirituality became prominent in the writings of the next few years.

Undoubtedly the great majority of the more recent 'peak

experiences' (to use Abraham Maslow's phrase), that have occurred since the 1970s, have been purely linguistic and not at all visual. They have been moments of intense religious excitement about language, poetical frenzies associated with particular metaphors, puns, felicitous phrases, reversals, ironies. But, on retrospective analysis, the visual experiences have also turned out without exception to be highly condensed, symbolic and language-formed. Reversing the normal way metaphors are thought of as working, intellectual light became a metaphor for natural light, and I saw something earthly, such as Rachel S——, the wistaria, and the glittering sunbeam, as if it were also heavenly and was well able to represent to me, respectively, an angel, eternal life and the divine glory. Something entirely natural showed itself to be already everything that the supernatural could possibly be. Even the experiences that seemed *prima facie* to be the most visual and least verbal were in fact highly condensed and languagey, anti-Platonic and this-worldly. They fused the heavenly and earthly worlds together: they taught what I have slowly learned to call 'ecstatic immanence'. From my earliest years, I was jumping ecstatically, not out of, but *back into* immanence. At such a moment we give up the multi-storey and stretched-out vision of the world, we give up the ugly and painful contrasts between here-Below and up-Above, and between Now and Then, and we give up all the illusions of metaphysical 'depth'. We give up everything and suddenly find eternal happiness, on the surface only and just Now, where Be-ing pours quietly forth into the dance of meanings and the flickering play of the most transient phenomena. That's bliss; it is 'the mysticism of secondariness', and it is what I am here calling the Revelation of Being – joyous acceptance of the way everything *turns out*, or just *happens to be*. It is high-speed ravishment, like lightning: it is sudden glory. It is what Carlyle calls 'natural supernaturalism'. It is eternal happiness, briefly, in and *with* the here and now.

The violent but very brief religious event of July 1997 that was described in the first paragraph of this Introduction was, as you should have noticed, also a purely natural event, a brainstorm. I described it as such: words crowd together and spark off each other, there is a build-up of tension in some kind of loop in the nervous system, a point of no return at which release begins, and then a joyful explosion. All of which makes my religious experiences into neurological events of just the same general type as sneezes, orgasms and fits. And why not? The sense of sight and the motion of language can have and do have that kind of violent effect upon us. Just words may send us, and blow our minds. Words can create and destroy us. So I was blown away by my momentary, oh-so-transient beatific vision of the outsideless, living and purely contingent three-in-one-and-one-in-three unity of Being, Man and Language. Philosophical bliss by jumping not out, but back in; not ecstasy but entostasy. A purely immanent, *for me*, living, moving unity of everything.

The neurological discharge, being so rapid and so 'deliriously' happy, seems to be fast carrying away the memory of the running sentences and complex arguments that led up to it. I've learnt that one must move quickly. So I took a pen and immediately wrote down the paragraph beginning 'At last, at last . . .', which was left to stand unrevised on p.146 of the published version of *The Religion of Being*. One must get something down at once that can serve as a starting-point for retrospective analysis. Then a week or two later I wrote the Inconclusion and gave the whole book a valedictory cast. Had I glimpsed my own final destination? Is the Religion of Being in the end unwritable? Was the valediction a necessary way of showing (not saying) why the book called *The Religion of Being* cannot go further than it does towards actually delivering the blessedness it describes? The text cannot do more than try to point to a language-happiness explosion that must of course remain off the page. We start to describe it only after we have already lost it.

The Revelation of Being

To make progress here, we must fasten tenaciously upon the one point that we are most tempted to overlook. We must understand that the feeling of having narrowly missed something infinitely important that slipped away too quickly to be grasped properly, and the feeling of extreme happiness, are not in themselves so very important. They were purely natural events in the brain, and as such are not to be trusted. What comes first and matters most is the complex many-stranded motion of language – or if you prefer, of signs – that led up to and then triggered off the psychological explosion. It is obvious enough that language does have huge psychological power over us, but these particular words and phrases were so exceptionally potent that they caused me actually to throw a fit with happiness. It's worth finding out *why*; it's worth trying to spread them all out, and trying to understand how it all worked and why it was so good. What we will find is that the build-up and the subsequent explosion was so complex a language-event that an adequate analysis of it must take the form of a whole system of thought. And such a system of thought will be a philosophy, or a religion – an account of the Way to Blessedness, or salvation, or release, or the Highest Good. It will not just explain bliss, but if sufficiently artfully ordered will guide the reader to bliss. It will show the way and it will be the Way.

We see now why Nietzsche surmises that every great system of philosophy is a spiritual autobiography. Many indeed of the great philosophers make it clear to us that their whole system and their entire argument has been constructed with but one end in view: they want to show us, explain to us, and help us to share in the special vision of things and state of soul in which they have found their own personal release and their highest happiness. This is true for example of Spinoza and Hume, Anselm and Erigena, Schopenhauer and Bradley and many others. The same is also true of those painters whose work most obviously expresses and seeks to share with us their own experience of visual joy as deserving to be called 'ultimate' or 'eternal' or 'religious' happiness: Turner, Monet, Cezanne, and Matisse, for example.

However, I don't think anybody previously has openly admitted to developing a whole text around a brief neurological episode that, considered simply as such, doesn't really amount to more than a sneeze. So let's do it. Let's spread it all out, and see if we can't create a literary effect of eternal happiness in slow motion. I mean, it might be even better if it is more long-drawn-out.

*　　*　　*

At this point I need to reply to the accusation that nowadays I'm inventing a new religion. To that, my reply is that we need to give up the idea of religions, in the plural, as a class. *A religion* is usually thought of as a distinct cultural system, vested in a distinct body of people. It is implied that there are many such objects, each with its own local roots and distinct tradition. Religions are thought of as being mutually-exclusive, like nationalisms: practising one of them, you are shutting-out all the others. Religion's job is to tell you who your brothers are, and who your enemies. But I argue that we need to give up that narrow, 'positive', conception of religion, and I admit only to being somebody who tries bit-by-bit to invent a universal-human kind of religion and then tries to give it away. What a useless thing to do.

2. Being

The first and founding question of philosophy, it has been claimed, is the question of being. How has the world come into being? What is it, *to be*? How are things able to *be*? What brings them into being? What *is* being, be-ing, anyway? What *is* there (in Greek: *ti on;*)? What is it to be in existence, in being? What is the *reason* for the existence of things, what is the *ground* of all being? How is it that all being is utterly contingent, (that is, just happpenstance), so that nothing is certain and anything or everything may at any moment cease to be – whilst yet at the same time Be-ing, the forthcoming of everything, turns out in the event to be so persistent, so gentle and reliable? Abyssal, terrifying contingency combined with sweetness and even moral constancy – and both at once! A world both random and pre-dictable, chaotic and orderly, uncanny and homely. A life that is at once sweet and frightening.

This seeming ambiguity has come to be widely recognized only in modern times, and still takes some getting used so. On the one hand everything in the world is contingent – just happens – and nothing has got to be, or is compelled to be just the way it is. There is indeed a lot of random about. But at the same time and on the medium scale probabilities and nature's habits work out in such a way that events (or some of them, at least) are predictable, the world steady and life sweet enough. The ambiguity remains, and is enough to account for the difference between, for example, Schopenhauer and Leibniz. Schopenhauer is typical of people who find the sheer anything-may-happen contingency of Being frightening. As a result, like so many men of his kind, he is both a misogynist and afraid of death. In the end there is for him only the Void, and the creative void that Woman carries inside her body frightens him. It makes him shake. Leibniz, on the other hand, is typical of those people who believe they can bring Being under the control of Reason. The Principle of Sufficient Reason assures Leibniz that he is entitled to put Being on the spot and demand that it give a full account of itself. In Leibniz's rationalist metaphysics, Being is obliged to justify itself, explain itself, excuse itself, and produce a rational Ground of itself. He tames it thoroughly, rationalizes it.

Thus Leibniz was the last great exponent of pure old-fashioned patriarchal rationalism. The thought of Being's constancy encouraged him to attempt a comprehensive subjection of Being to Reason and a proof that the universe which results is the best of all possible worlds. In the long run, and for the God's-eye-view, everything is rational, everything makes sense, and everything is for the best.

Schopenhauer, by contrast, was the first great exponent of late-modern and postmodern nihilism and pessimism. The thought of Being's pure contingency led him to conclude that *of course* life does not make sense. In the long run we have no defence against the suffering and death that await us all, except calm resignation, the consolations of art, and the renunciation of the will to live. Our being reflects, or suffers, the turbulent play of the irrational unconscious forces that in turn make us, make sport of us, and then unmake us. And that's that. We emerge from Nothing, we are tossed about, and then we come to Nothing again.

We shall not here be following either Leibniz or Schopenhauer. We'll take them both instead as offering a moral lesson in the extent to which even a great philosophical system is a psychological projection, an enlarged self-portrait. It has been said of the film actress Ingrid Bergmann that the secret of her great power was her ability on screen to keep still and let the audience make all the running. In a big scene she can be motionless, sweet and pensive with just the faintest quiver, widening of the eyes or catch of breath – and she has us hooked. We project upon her our feelings and our dreams. We make her into what we want her to be for us. And so it is with Being. Being itself is an unthinkable unthing prior to language, a non-word, ~~Being~~. It is pure outpouring, slipping, formless, malleable contingency. Pure random, pure flitting, a dance of possibility in the Void.[1] Sweet and amenable, it waits for our language to make something of it. Think of it, perhaps, as coming at you like a gentle breath of wind, an insufflation in your face. In your mouth your tongue will form that breath into a sentence, which you will send out as the vehicle and the executant of your meaning and your will.

Think of Being, in a word, as ventilating events; as a very light wind, a 'gentle gale' or fountain of pure hap that upholds and supports everything that happens. It is the happening-to-turn-out-as-they-do of all things. It is awesome, abyssal, sometimes terrifying – but also easy and gentle. Language always presupposes it, but must always lose it in and *by* grasping it. We actively sign and impress all the time: we project ourselves out, we impress ourselves upon, we appropriate for ourselves and we remake things, all in our own image; and as we do this, we are so bloody determined to impose our will that we forget and lose Being. As Bergmann (rather cunningly) allows us to make what we want of her, so Being allows us to make what we want of it, and with it. Being is so sweet we lose it. It goes along with us unnoticed, like one's own shadow.

As you'll gather, I am linking the forgetting of Being with the victory of light over darkness, of order over chaos, and therewith the triumph of patriarchal reason and the subjection of Woman, and I am linking pessimism and nihilism with the dread of Woman as representing to us all the contingency, vulnerability, emptiness and death that we dread. When we idealize woman we are attempting, by making her ours, by shackling her to us, to liberate her from the vulnerability and mortality which we nevertheless unconsciously recognize in her and fear that we have ourselves contracted from her. (And remember that I am here talking not just of the attitude of man to woman, but of the deeper and even more potent feeling that there is in both sexes towards the body of the mother. She who gave us life therewith also gave us our death. Being is for all of us our M/Other.) Our forgetting of Being is thus not an oversight. We *struggle* to forget Being; we hasten to master it and to transform it into our own image in the hope of overcoming the abyssal dread and terror that it arouses in us. If you doubt me, be honest with yourself: never before has it occurred to you that your mother gave you your death.

A corollary of this present argument is that one of the historic functions of the Fear of God was to conquer and deliver us from the older, and even greater and more terrible Fear of Being. In the ancient mythologies, Being is represented by original Darkness or Chaos, by the Primal Waters, and by a female watermonster such as Nessie, Grendel or Tiamat. Being is associated with darkness and unconsciousness, because it is prior to language. The masculine divinity conquers this darkness, slaying the monster and filling the world with light by the power of his spoken utterance. God thus becomes established authority enthroned over the waters, as in so many of the Hebrew Psalms. The Fear of God thenceforth is the fear and dread of established and victorious absolute authority, holiness, power and perfection. It is *respect*, a duty we owe.

By contrast, the Fear of Being is the far greater and older fear of the radically outsideless contingency and transience of all existence. Biblically, it is the fear of drowning, of being overwhelmed by 'the waters'. It is fear of the zero, the cavemouth from which we have come, and fear of life's irremediable groundlessness and insecurity. Our whole existence is absurd, gratuitous, *de trop*.

The Revelation of Being

Suppose that we follow Nietzsche's hint in dating the Death of God around the year 1800 CE, and link it with such events as the French Revolution, the 'Atheism Controversy' that was sparked off in Germany by the dismissal of J.G. Fichte from his chair of philosophy at Jena in 1799, and also the first publication of Schopenhauer's *The World as Will and as Idea* in 1818. Then it will not be surprising to find that the spiritual history of the nineteenth and twentieth centuries has been deeply influenced by a revived Fear of Being. In a great deal of Romantic and Symbolist art, for example, Woman is seen as a fearsome and threatening figure who is associated with death: Medusa, Salome, Judith, Hecate. A whole series of relatively-novel words become prominent: *Angst* or dread, pessimism, *ennui*, nihilism, *anomie*.[2] There is a crisis of authority, and a confused struggle either to reconnect with the past (traditionalism, nationalism, roots, identity, fundamentals) or to find some new authority strong enough to reconquer the Fear of Being.

In the generation of Heidegger, Sartre and Camus the old pessimistic Fear of Being was still strong; but since the 1960s it has become clear that everything is now changed. Biology is at last becoming the leading science, which is good for Woman and good for the values of the Religion of Being. We are giving up the last traces of belief in life after death, and therewith giving up also the old and foolish fear of death. You feel and I feel an increasingly strong religious love for everything short-lived, watery, once-only, volatile, ephemeral, shadowy, trembling, emotional and briefly-glimpsed. The more bloody Plato scorns it, the more I love it. What's most fleeting is what best reveals Being: the Revelation of Being as love depends upon, and is intimately linked with, religious acceptance of *one's own* transience.

3. Man

The special sense in which I am using the word 'Man' is a little difficult to grasp, but of great importance. It is difficult, perhaps because to this day Anglo-Saxon individualism remains such a powerful influence upon our thinking. It leads us habitually to make an oddly false and misleading distinction between the individual human being and her world, her milieu, and her playing of her various roles in life. This in turn leaves us with far too contracted a notion of 'Man', the *Humanum*. It is as if the influence of science, with its ideal of the dispassionate, disengaged observer, has reached back into the world of everyday life and has led us almost habitually to picture ourselves as creatures who look at our own life and our own world from an ideal standpoint somewhere outside it. This may give us the idea that the real self is a spectator of life, existing in a world of pure thought prior to and apart from its own embeddedness in society and history – and it has to be said that in our postmodern entertainment culture we are all too ready to see ourselves as mere spectators of life, watchers rather than actors. We thus oddly detach the human self from the human world. And in very much the same way, the distinctions we draw between the various sciences – psychology, sociology, biology, physical science – also seem to have worked their way back into the world of everyday life, leading us to draw over-sharp lines between the individual and society, between man and animal, and between Culture and Nature. Thus the distinctions that we draw between subject-areas may suggest to us that the human realm – the world of everyday life and of human history – is only a sub-world within the larger world of Nature. We tend to forget and even to deny the extent to which our language, our interpretation, our construction of things runs everywhere, shaping everything and appropriating everything into the human realm. As an important but recently-neglected philosopher wrote in 1844: 'Man is no abstract being squatting outside the world. Man is the world of man, the State, Society'.[1]

At least since the time of Locke, however, Anglo-Saxons have commonly esteemed natural science more highly than philosophy. Philosophy's job is not to criticize natural science but to be its apologist and its 'under-labourer', to quote Locke's term. As a result we tend to approve most strongly of those philosophers whose temper is closest to our own scientific and empiricist turn of mind – which means that we prefer Aristotle, Lucretius, Descartes, Locke, Hume and Mill. And we have therefore been very slow to accept the widening of the notion of 'Man' and the human realm that has taken place in philosophy since Kant, Hegel and Marx. But the effect of their work – hard though it remains for us Anglo-Saxons to grasp and accept the point – has been gradually to undercut the distinction between *our* world and *the* world. The objective world around us is, all the way down, a world that *we ourselves* have formed, described, theorized, appropriated, constructed. The world is always already *our* world, a world that we have spread ourselves over, familiarized, appropriated. We get to know things by making them ours.

Anglo-Saxon commentators upon Kant are often a little ill-at-ease at this point, the point where he speaks of Nature as 'made by the mind'. We make the world in our knowing of it just as in ancient religious myths gods create the world, whether by imposing form upon clay with their hands, or upon chaos with their utterance. Kant's point is that for there to be intelligible experience *at all* the confused raw data of experience have to be brought by us under general rules and concepts. We give all the orders and we fill in all the meanings, everywhere. The world you see is the world we made. Humans are after all the only beings whose communication-system, and therefore whose consciousness, is sufficiently evolved for them to have a complete world. Think of it: nobody but us has a world *at all*.

The way we make the world may be compared with the way energetic colonists a few centuries ago arrived in nameless, trackless, virgin territory where there was 'nothing', as one might say, and promptly set about mapping it, opening up communications routes, establishing settlements, naming everything, imposing the rule of Law, and so on. Setting aside modern reservations about colonialism, it is the case that in only about a century and a half these energetic people built major countries, where previously there had been only a very thinly-populated wilderness. In some such way humankind generally over many, many millennia has gradually evolved all of our languages, our forms of consciousness, our knowledge-systems, our technologies and, in short, our world. We have evolved our world as a habitable theatre, a stage on which we can live. And nobody else but us has done this: that is why the only world there yet is is the human world, our world. The world known is the world we own.

In all of our experience we are projecting out our own language – our general notions, our interpretations, our feelings and our evaluations – upon the featureless flux of Forthcoming. Our vocabulary does still reflect the way in which the ordered intelligible world of experience is produced by our actively putting a construction upon an input of raw formless data. Consider the difference between mere looking and actually *seeing* something, and between mere listening and actually *hearing* something. As the idioms show, interpretation confers objectivity, and builds a world. As we descry and discern things, we *make* them *out*. World-builders, we make the contents of our own visual field, and set them out there as part of our world. 'Make out' equals objecti-fy. Looking plus language equals seeing something, listening plus language equals hearing a noise that actually *means* something. In this latter case, the terms we use show how the application of signs to the raw flux both produces things and bestows significance.

Along with Idealist philosophy, we should think of the world of mind as being in the first place the public realm, the communications-network where language flies about, meanings are established, and the world is built. Your mind, to quote an old saying, is not behind but in front of your face. The Mind is not an archipelago, a collection of distinct islands of mentality, one inside each person's skull, but rather it is the common air which we all breathe. It is our ordered human public world, the world of our shared consciousness, out there. There is nothing intelligible inside your skull; rather, what is intelligible is the rapid motion of signs over your exterior surface – your words, your body-language, the signals you give off. I read your mind by reading your exterior, not by probing your interior. Your mind is your self-expression, your angle upon and your participation in the common world of symbolic exchange. As for your inwardness and your Unconscious, they are not hidden within your interior, but rather are *also* legible in the form of a subtext on your exterior, as when your body-language is at odds with your spoken words.

In the case of looks and looking there is an interestingly delicate interaction between different sorts of look. Not only do I look out enquiringly upon the world to see what's to be seen, but also things out there have looks, and look *to me*. She's good-looking, you look bored, it looks like rain, what are you *looking for?* 'Looking' may be several different things: presenting an appearance, searching, enquiring, signifying and so on. The startlingly-complex logic of looks and looking indicates to us the way in which the common world is the complex shifting product both of the co-operation *and of the competition* between a variety of different viewpoints, interests, and interpretations.

Man

All these considerations indicate why it is that, at least in European philosophy since Hegel, the world of 'Man' – that is, the world of language, culture and history – tends with increasing force and clarity to *precede and enclose* the world of Nature. The Universe is a little bit of us, rather than vice versa. We made our world, and within it, more recently, we made 'the Universe'.

Suppose we ask: 'How old are the galaxies?' Anglo-Saxon scientific realism promptly replies: 'They began to form very early on in the history of the Universe – around 15×10^9 years ago'. But from the point of view of 'Man' the answer is: 'About 75 years. The transition from a single-galaxy universe, in which the word "galaxy" just meant the Milky Way, to a multi-galaxy universe took place gradually through the controversies of the 1920s'. Old-fashioned commonsensical Anglo-Saxons who put science first are apt to find all answers of this second type intensely irritating. But from the point of view of philosophy it is important to remember that 'science is a humanity'; that every scrap of our scientific world-picture is an intra-linguistic and intra-historical construct; and that we cannot separate the way the world is absolutely from the way our current theory represents it. From these considerations it follows that the galaxies too are part of 'Man' – by which I mean human being, *Dasein*, situated within and surrounded by its own historically-evolving human world.

Galaxies have a history in language. *Gala* (genitive, *galaktos*) is milk in Greek. 'The Galaxy' was still simply the Milky Way in the *Oxford English Dictionary* volume of 1901. But Galileo himself had almost three centuries earlier observed a class of small objects that appeared *nebulous*, *smudgy,* as if they were *clouds of dust*. Improved telescopes showed some of them to be of *spiral* form, as if they were rotating like Catherine wheels. This vocabulary already suggests the possibility of the Kant-Laplace 'nebular hypothesis' of 1755, accounting for the formation of the solar system. But a huge further theoretical leap has been made when it comes to be argued that the Milky Way is itself a nebula, made not of dust but of millions of stars, and seen by us who are inside it in transverse section; in which case the objects that had long been described as *nebulae* can be renamed *galaxies*, like our own.

In mythology the Milky Way might be seen, right up to the extravagant canvas by Tintoretto, as having been splashed from the full breast of a goddess. Thereafter, the layman's *smudge* becomes classical astronomy's *nebula*, and modern astronomy's *galaxy*. And these verbal changes mark big theoretical shifts in what is *seen* by the astronomer who looks through a telescope. Seeing is shaped by words, which in turn bring theories with them.

With this familiar example from astronomy in mind, we can now make a whole string of general statements. One may look and look, but one only *sees* when one can recognize and tell, or describe, or bear witness to, what one sees. That is, in all intelligible experience the proximate object is not a sense-datum or sense-impression, as the empiricists used to say, but simply a sign. The object understood is always and only the sign. The sign makes experience intelligible and conscious because of its generality: it invokes connections with other occasions in the past when it has been activated, and in the future when it may be reactivated. So the field of view is also the field of consciousness, which is the world of language, which is the human world.

Look at it, before you now! Everything you see or hear you can describe, straight off and at high speed, because perception itself is already language-mediated. You read the world before you, as you read the expressions on your friend's face as you watch her speaking, and as you read the signs of the times. The world is all 'Man', all human, and nothing in it is wholly alien to us – which gives an interesting twist to the ancient humanist's boast *Nihil humanum a me alienum puto*: I deem nothing human alien to me. Everything human is (in principle) friendly and intelligible, and there is nothing that is quite *non*-human. Our ancestors used to be a prey to all manner of superstitious terrors because they feared that the world was partly defined and controlled by a menagerie of fearsome non-human agents such as ghosts, spirits, gods, monsters and the like. But there cannot for us be any such beings, because we are the only makers of language, and therefore the only makers of the/our world. There is no non-human speech, there is no non-human intelligibility, no non-human agency and no wholly non-human world. We can forget the old distinction between what is wild and what has been domesticated. *Everything* is now homely, and there is nothing uncanny. It's all yours – I mean, *really* all yours; and you have nothing to fear. The first redemption is the realization that nothing non-human makes the world, and there is nothing non-human to be afraid of.

From this it appears that our prime religious concern henceforth is not with anything numinous and dreadful that crops up within the human world – there is no such thing – but simply with Being. That is, we need to relate ourselves aright to life's pure outpouring contingency, to Nothingness, and to death. If we can relate ourselves aright to Being, we ought to be able to live without anxiety, without covetousness and without fear. We ought to be able to say a whole-hearted Yes to life. That is the second redemption, just now becoming available to us.

Older ideas of redemption often centred upon ideas of sin and ritual pollution and their consequences. Being was objectified as God, and credited with absolute power and authority. God had originally laid down and would enforce the ritual and moral framework, prescribed by tradition, within which human life ought to be lived. There were rules to be observed and lines that must not be crossed. The universal human impulse to break the Law was attributed to a proud, rebellious and uppity streak inherent in human nature since the Fall. To be safe and to be saved one needed forgiveness of the sins one had already committed, and also an inner moral transformation that would protect one against the will to commit more sins in the future.

Under the old dispensation, then, what one most needed to be saved from was a presumptuous will-to-disobedience within oneself that led one deliberately to commit the disastrous error of offending against absolute perfection, authority and power. The inevitable result would be everlasting and total ruin and damnation, unless one could find forgiveness and absolution.

Just to spell out this whole circle of ideas, once so vivid and powerful, is to realize how completely they have faded away. The Fear of God is now a rarity. It has been replaced by the Fear of Being – the fear aroused in us by life's radical insecurity, the groundlessness of everything; the fear of finitude and temporality; the fear of the way everything steadily slips away towards oblivion. This Fear leads us to clutch greedily and desperately at all manner of idols – 'absolutes', 'certainties', authorities. We need to be cured of it, so that we can learn to live expressively, as the Sun does. And a large part of the cure comes when we fully understand the humanity of Being: there *is* no radically non-human reality. Man – that is, the human world, the world that we humans have reached out to, described, theorized, and taken into our language – is Being's expression, and the world of Man is the only world. It is entirely possible and reasonable to be completely happy with things just as they are.

At this point many people want to bring up the problem of evil against me. Am I being unduly optimistic, and glossing over the well-known facts of physical and moral evil (suffering and sin)? In reply, let me repeat what I have said before: that my argument is directed principally against what Leibniz described as 'metaphysical evil', which means not just finitude and limitation, but the very idea that there is something unsatisfactory, wrong, and beyond our power to rectify, in the human condition as such. Some such idea as this has played a very large part in both Buddhist and Latin Christian thought ever since late antiquity. It has led to the feeling that we don't really belong here, and to a picture of our whole life as a Long March through the wilderness, 'pilgrims through this barren land'.

In reply, I say that the Revelation of Being involves a dramatic revaluation precisely of contingency and transience. Getting rid of the idea of metaphysical evil makes a huge difference to our whole view of life and what we can do with it.

* * *

Your mind, I said, is your self-expression, your angle upon and your participation in the common world of symbolic exchange. To read your mind and to make judgments about your psychology, I don't need to perform a craniotomy and take a look inside your skull; I need only interpret your behaviour, your body-language and what you say. Especially your *social* behaviour, your intercourse with others; for if we consider examples from drama, we will probably agree that dialogue is usually more informative psychologically than is soliloquy. When I give you a piece of my mind, I give myself away: look at the idioms!

The question now arises of how, and how well, we can know ourselves. Is our knowledge of ourselves better and more intimate than our knowledge of other people can ever be; or is it rather the case that we have a very unsatisfactory view of ourselves and do not see ourselves at all clearly? In our earlier discussion I have gone a long way towards simply identifying the field of consciousness with the visual field, and the view of ourselves which the visual field gives us is very far from satisfactory. With an effort of attention I can see the orbit of my eye, the tip of my nose, an eyebrow, and – looking down – most of the front of my body. I have a fair amount of internal sensation reporting the state of my body, the position of my limbs and so forth. And I know that I do not just look into my visual field, but that I am bodily situated in it, and able to move around it. But apart from that, my legible self is tucked discreetly away and becomes a rather shadowy Magritte-like figure on the near side of the visual field. I don't see my own face and my own body language, and during a close conversation I have a much better view of what the other person is saying and meaning than I have of my own contribution.

In Warsaw there used to be a rather obvious joke about the huge Stalinist monument that dominated the city from the 1950s on: 'What's the best place from which to see Warsaw?' Answer: 'The Palace of Culture, because it is the only place in Warsaw from which you can't see the Palace of Culture'. The self is a little like that: the self that is the subject of consciousness is not one of the objects of consciousness, and the eye does not get a good view of itself. I am tucked away unobtrusively on the near side of the visual field, like the self-effacing narrator of many a nineteenth-century novel, who is in the story observing and reporting to the reader all the events of the story, without ever coming into clear view himself.

In his famous discussion of personal identity, David Hume uses the old language of introspection. He finds, on looking within himself, that we have no constant and unvarying first-hand 'impression' of ourselves:

> For my part, when I enter most intimately into what I call myself, I always stumble on some particular perception or other, of heat or cold, light or shade, love or hatred, pain or pleasure. I never catch *myself* at any time without a perception, and never can observe any thing but the perception. When my perceptions are remov'd for any time, as by sound sleep; so long am I insensible of *myself*, and may truly be said not to exist . . .[2]
>
> They are the successive perceptions only, that constitute the mind; nor have we the most distant notion of the place where these scenes are represented, or of the materials of which it is composed.[3]
>
> The identity, which we ascribe to the mind of man, is only a fictitious one, and of a like kind with that which we ascribe to vegetables and animal bodies.[4]

Man

When Hume thinks about the self, he thinks about the mind as a sort of inner theatre through which passes a flux of perceptions, each of which is a distinct little sense-datum, or feeling. And he finds that there is no constant and unvarying perception of the self. The self, it seems, is elusive; its unity is a fictioned unity, like that of a nation or an organism.

We are coming to a conclusion rather similar to Hume's, but by a very different route. We don't look for the self in the inner world of subjectivity as Hume did; we look for it out in the common world of symbolic exchange. The visual field itself we do not see as made of atomic visual impressions, or *qualia*, or *data*. So far as it is intelligible, legible and describable, we are seeing the visual field as a field of *signs* in motion. (Consider here another vivid idiom: *Mind out!*) And when we consider the visual field as a field of signs in motion, where is the self? It is elusive again: each of us finds it much easier to read other persons than it is to read oneself. I don't have at all a good idea of my own body-language. I don't read myself well. The self is a relatively minor and nondescript character, weak and even empty, like some 'I-person' narrators in novels.

Here we reach a point that is made strongly both by Heidegger and by the Buddhists. The withdrawal of the self opens up the visual field or the field of discourse, allowing other beings room to stand out, bright and clear. As in the Victorian novel the narrator assures us that he was present at all the events and reports them truthfully, but effaces himself[5] so as not to get in the way and thereby makes the events of the novel stand out all the more solid and believable – so it is with the human self and the human world.[6] Consider the way a skilled and sympathetic interviewer effaces herself in order to *draw out* the subject of the interview, to the point where she does no more than give the lightest of touches to the conversational steering-wheel – and *it all comes out.* This particular kind of delicacy is called 'humility' in Western religion, and *anatta* (no-self) in Eastern religion. It is also the scientific attitude.

Elsewhere it has been described as the state of being 'lost in the objectivity of world-love'.

We need a certain religious tact and delicacy in order to *draw out* other things and people, and allow them to real-ize themselves. We are not the masters of our world, or of language, or of Being. In our relation to *each* we need to learn and to practise a discipline of attention and mutuality, rather as in dancing with a partner.

It is necessary to emphasize this point in order to distinguish our religious humanism from something that is often confused with it, namely the Self-infatuation that troubled a good deal of European philosophy between Rousseau and Sartre.[7]

Our religious humanism does not involve any return to supernatural belief. We still insist that we are the only makers of our world; nothing but us shapes it all. And it is religiously profoundly liberating to be finally delivered from all forms of fear of the supernatural, the unknown, the uncanny. There is nothing of that sort, because – to quote the most dazzlingly-simple argument of all – we invented every word in the language. *Every natural language is a complete world, and we invented every bit of every natural language.* That is conclusive. But, religious humanism goes on to say, we will not make a good world by asserting ourselves and throwing our weight about. On the contrary, we should relate ourselves to Being, to Language and to our world as amenable partners. Let it be.

4. Language

Philosophy may begin with Being, with Man or with Language. Ancient philosophy typically began with being, and in Aristotle and elsewhere moved on to man and language via the image of a speaker or craftsman whose utterance or manual skill imposes form upon formless being or stuff, in order to make particular beings. Modern philosophy, from Descartes, typically began with man, the individual subject who as he speaks defines himself, and builds his world. Postmodern philosophy begins simply with language, or even just the linguistic sign.[1] The 'thrust' or expressive force of language reveals the speaker-subjects who are using the language, and in what it accomplishes language reveals the world they build. Thus Being comes forth via language into the being of humans and their world. 'Man' is the realm in which, and language is the means by which, Being comes to light.

Philosophy, then, may begin with Being, with Man, or with Language; but whichever it begins with, it will work its way towards the other two.

Today, for good reasons that are to do with the way philosophy has developed since the Enlightenment and the Romantic movement, we begin with language. If philosophy could still be thought of as having one proper starting-point, then that starting-point would have to be language. Because language is the medium in which philosophy is done, it should be philosophy's first topic. And we should be wary of any appeal to intuition of something extra-linguistic. Why? – because nothing extra-linguistic can be meaningful or can be understood. We think in language – in two senses, because signs are the coinage of thinking, and because language supplies the entire milieu or space within which thinking moves. By 'language' I mean not just one or more of our natural languages, but also our other specialized, artificial sign-systems; and we think in language, I say, and we understand only language. There is no understanding of anything at all except the general signs that connect the here and now with other actual and possible occasions. All perception involves the activation of words, through which I recognize what I'm looking at. In my present field of view words including window, sky, overcast, trees, elms, buildings, cars, grass, people, are being activated. Language, human language, is the ubiquitous, subtle, free-ranging formative and vitalizing 'principle' that moves over everything. It is outsideless, it is everywhere. It is exactly and precisely what in antiquity and in religion has been called the Logos, the Tao, and Wisdom, and even also Torah and Dharma. Why? – because these terms described expressions of the Divine Mind; and, like us, God was supposed to think in language. The world was pervaded by God's expressed utterance. Wisdom is, in C.H. Dodd's words, 'the hypostatized thought of God projected in creation, and remaining as an immanent power within the world and in man'[2] – that is, in modern terms, simply language. For the coextensiveness of the world and language, and the construction of all reality within language and by the motion of language, is exactly and precisely the modern version of the traditional idea of the omnipresence within the world of the formative and life-giving divine Word, or Spirit, or Wisdom. Postmodern philosophy is an interesting secularization, and perhaps a scattering or a 'dissemination', of the traditional theological vision of the world. For 'the Holy Spirit' read simply 'words'.

You may ask why the ubiquitous, world-forming creative activity that we now attribute simply to language was in former times attributed to the divine Word or Spirit? I suggest that there are certain features of language which in the past appeared to demand a supernatural explanation of it. In an important logical or philosophical sense, language precedes us. It is older than we are, and it has made us ourselves. We were inducted into it, and became ourselves within it. Secondly, there is also an important sense in which language is auto-mobile. It runs by itself: it speaks us as much as we speak it. For example, in order to be a creative thinker, you do not screw up your eyes and work hard at thinking: on the contrary, you just set two or three words and phrases in place and then lie back and free-associate. Relax. Do nothing. Let your mind wander, *diverge*. Just let language run, and watch passively to see what it comes up with. When something good crops up, name it out loud so that it gets remembered. Jot it down. That's thinking. It's so easy that very few people have ever bothered with it. Thirdly, language is indeed a universal creative and formative principle, just like the Sun in Plato's allegory. It lights up everything, gives to each thing a clear outline, makes everything intelligible and so gives to us this common world that is before our eyes.

So language precedes us; and it is describable both as being auto-mobile like spirit, and as being the universal creator. In so far as it is ubiquitous but invisible, it may like spirit (*pneuma, anima*) be compared with the wind; insofar as it heaves and moves restlessly, it has traditionally been compared with the sea; and insofar as it lights up the world and makes everything intelligible, it may be compared with the Sun. Given all this, it is not surprising that in traditional thought the powers of language seemed supernatural and were referred to God. People thought of God as a language-user, as the first speaker, as having made the world by speaking over the Void, as having taught language to the first human beings, and as having begotten in his heart from all eternity his supreme and final Word to humankind. And people were not wrong to think these things, provided one makes due allowance for the difference between a traditional society in which God personifies the authority of tradition and commands us to keep all meanings, truths and values unchanged, and an historical society like our own, in which meanings, truths and values evolve continuously in and through the daily interactions of human speakers. In traditional society everything is thought of as having been laid down in the beginning by the power of God, who thereafter acts to maintain intact the order he has established. Insofar as the auto-mobile and innovative powers of language, moving within humans, are recognized, they are described in terms of prophecy and glossolalia, and are attributed to divine inspiration. In our own historical type of society there is no antecedently-established order with special authority at all; instead, everything is seen as historically-evolving. We emerge within what at first sight may seem to be a ready-made world. After a few decades of life we recognize that it is in fact the accumulated deposit of the human past; but much though we may wish to respect it, in everything we say, think, do or judge, we are criticizing, revaluing and modifying our heritage. And that is how it has to be. The world is always in process of being made and is never finished. It can never be finished.

The sense in which language is auto-mobile, like soul in Plato, also calls for some further explanation. The world of language – the world of signs – is a finite-but-unbounded world of flowing, interconnected meanings. All meaning is differential, and therefore *immanent;* that is, internal to the world of language. Pointing, naming, and referring should not be thought of as operations that tie language down to a supposed extra-linguistic 'Reality'. On the contrary, these operations are performed within language, and all theories of 'Reality' are of course themselves also intra-linguistic constructs.

These considerations may help us to see why von Humboldt defined language as 'an activity',[3] and why the distinction between 'living' and 'dead' languages is so important. The ability of a natural language to name things, to describe a world and to function as the medium of a people's life depends upon its being in constant circulation, and *itself* subject to change.

People long found the implications of this hard to grasp, no doubt because Western culture and education were for so long dominated by the study of dead languages. It was hard to grasp that a one-language dictionary of a living natural language cannot pretend to be more than a snapshot of a moment in the life of a living, moving organism.

5. Being and Man

As we have been saying, classical philosophy usually started from the question of Being. Modern philosophy began with Man, and with the task of justifying our trust in our new and humanly-constructed knowledge, world-view, ethics and civil society. Postmodern philosophy, in the most communicative era there has ever been, naturally begins with Language, or even simply with the Sign. So why don't we here follow those other postmodern philosophers who have thriftily taken the whole agenda of traditional philosophy under just one new heading – the Philosophy of the Sign? Josef Simon, perhaps the most economical postmodernist, seems to derive everything just from the sign, chains of signs, and the distinction between those signs that pass without comment and those signs that need to be followed by further signs explaining them or interpreting them.[1] Wouldn't it be good to be able to build a world and everything in it out of such simple constituents?

No – and for various reasons. The sign might become a new *arché*, First Principle or foundation; and the philosophy of the sign might then turn into a relaunch of metaphysics, or even theology.[2] It might turn out to be one of those explanatory theories that is too simple: because it explains too much too fast, people are left with a feeling that not very much really useful explaining has been done after all. Anyway, should we not demand a naturalistic explanation of the sign itself?

Hence my preference here for the triad, Being, Man and Language. They are very different in status. But they all merge in the Fountain. They enfold each other. They are different 'modes', or maybe different possible starting-points. None of them is an 'absolute', or can be viewed as the One Foundation of everything else. They are all finite, contingent, and temporally flowing. None of them can ever be quite still. And any one of them can if we wish be written out of the script, by being explained or explained away in terms of the others. So in our present picture there really *are* no absolutes, and nothing is posited as being primitive or ultimate or foundational. Everything is groundless. Everything can be explained, or explained away if you wish, in terms of everything else. I'm as happy about the fact that anything and everything can be *explained* away as I am about the fact that everything *passes* away.

Suddenly now the happiness returns: in the old philosophies one sought happiness in contemplating something that was eternally, necessarily and self-subsistently One. In It, everything was locked together in rational, systematic unity. But in the unity of Being, Man and Language in the Fountain that we see, there really are no necessities and no absolutes. There is no absolute Being, and no absolute Nothingness. There is just the outflow: of Be-ing as an efflux of pure formless possibility, of Language which calls Being out into concrete expression, and of Man – that is, the historically unfolding human world, the world of human symbolic exchange, the world of consciousness. Everything is interwoven, everything interacts, everything can be explained in terms of everything else, everything is only contingent, everything is in time, everything flows, everything is comically secondary like the Cheshire Cat's grin, and everything just happens to turn out or befall as it does.

The old religious object, self-subsistent, eternal and necessary Being, was sought by people who were stricken by the Fear of Be-ing – or rather, perhaps, of Be(com)ing. The religious object had to be such as to deliver them from, by taking them right out of, the changes and changes of this mortal life. But the Revelation of Be-ing makes me happy to be bound up with everything just the way it is. Somehow, everything is merely secondary and contingent; but somehow everything hangs together, in a living, changing and almost *organic* unity of which you and I are parts; and I'm content with that.

Part of religion is a feeling for the way one belongs to the whole. That, if you like, is the new version of the old 'doctrine of creation'. But, and more particularly, religion is about the way we relate ourselves to Being; and this, we will find, is the new version of the old 'doctrine of redemption'. From our past we have inherited a deep Fear of Being, which we associate with weakness, contingency, vulnerability, emptiness and death, and symbolically with Woman. During the long millennia of agricultural civilization we tended to see Woman and Nature as unreliable and needing to be governed by a transcendent and sovereign principle of patriarchal rationality: the Law of the Father, the King, God. This supreme and eternal controlling Authority stabilized life, and for a long period was fairly successful in repressing the Fear of Be-ing. But since the Enlightenment the gradual fading of the old central patriarchy has been accompanied by a revived Fear of Being. Our religious problem now is to remember and relearn Being, converting the old Fear of Being into a new religion of Being.

The relation of Man to Being is interestingly intermediate between autonomy and heteronomy, and I need to explain how and why.

Being (equals B̶e̶i̶n̶g̶, Be-ing, Be(com)ing) is not a substance. It is the remainder that language never quite gets hold of. The evolving Universe, *minus* even the completest possible mathematical description of it, equals Being. Any actual thing, minus even the completest account of it, equals Being. Being – equals B̶e̶i̶n̶g̶, Be-ing, Be(com)ing – is the unthing prior to language that our language always presupposes but can never describe; for as soon as language has latched on to it and formed it into some particular thing, it is lost. Being is pure contingent forthcomingness, possibility waiting to be actualized. In the old

38

mythologies it is something like Chaos, or the Primal Waters, or the original Dark. The Greeks thought of it as *aoristos* and *apeiros*, indeterminate and boundless: it gave them the shivers. Always, at the back of everything, there is something abyssal, dark, watery and uncontrollable that people dread.

Why is Being abyssal and terrifying? People are frightened of Death and the Void. People are frightened by the thought of their own happening to come into being in the darkness of the womb. People are just occasionally knocked sideways by the realization of life's utter contingency, and the utter precariousness of their own hold upon life, health, sanity and fortune.

I suspect that our difficulty arises from the fact that we are not yet fully accustomed to the relatively modern idea that everything is a matter of probabilities and that one must learn to live happily with risk. We tend to suppose that for everything to stay in place, the world must be fully determined and governed by physical necessity. Either we and everything else are subject to the absolute government of an Almighty God who has predetermined everything (heteronomy), or God's throne is vacant and we must ourselves take his place and assume his sovereignty (autonomy). If we are not up to it, the third possibility is simply nihilism. Emotionally, we are still inclined to be cosmic monarchists. We assume that someone or something must be in charge: a supreme Lawgiver is needed, to be the keystone or the Centre that holds everything together. Either God occupies that position, or Man does, or we are stuck in nihilism.

The religion of Being offers another possibility (ontonomy?). Being is not any thing. It is not a law. It is no kind of certainty or Absolute. It is gentle, sweet, amenable, purely-contingent forthcomingness. To live with it is a matter of accepting the element of risk and probability in life. One can learn to live easy with it despite occasional doldrums, just as sailors used to live with, co-operate with and wait upon the winds. Think of Being as the partner. Give up ideas of mastery, either way. Being is still the religious object, but now *minus* all ideas of *weight*, unconditional authority and mastery. Copying theism, our technologies normally seek totally-reliable control of nature. Learning the religion of Being might be compared with giving up diesel engines and learning to sail again, or giving up fossil-fuel power stations and learning instead to rely upon wind and water for energy. Total control and predictability can be given up. And so it might be in religion and in belief. We might learn that it is possible to *trust to luck*, combining faith with *un*certainty in a Universe that is no longer deterministic, but has become probabilistic all the way down. Being then is just a process of quantum fluctuation, a dance of probabilities, a breath that waits for some kind of container to flow into and fill.

In traditional religious thought, in the West at least, the religious object was compared with a rock, or a mighty fortress (*Ein' feste Burg*). One should have faith only in what was completely reliable and trustworthy. The heavenly City was constructed entirely of gold and jewels.[3] Nothing could be good or blessed unless it was solidly-founded and incorruptible.

But when Being becomes our Other and the religious object, all that is changed radically. We now say a religious Yes to everything changeable and chancy. We now prefer levity and mobility – even effervescence, rather than rock-like stolidity. Nothing is eternal, nothing is absolute, everything comes and goes. It is now twilight. Clouds sail slowly past my window, changing shape as they go. A flock of starlings wheel beneath the new moon. Inside, there is a copper-eyed green lacewing sitting on the wall. It reminds me that life affirms itself most purely and intensely in the frailest and most shortlived of creatures. Being's gentle, temporal, probabilistic forthcoming-ness is the condition of life, of consciousness, and also of course of death. It is all one: Amen to that.

6. Being and Language

Philosophy, I have been saying, needs to learn to do without a number of its long-cherished assumptions. It needs to forget the idea that the Universe has a ready-made intelligible structure and its own final vocabulary – presumably 'mentalese', as Plato seems to suppose – out there and waiting to be tapped into and copied down by us. There is no such thing as *getting it just right*. There is no final Truth, either about ourselves or about anything else. So we should give up philosophical 'scientism', or 'scholasticism' – the idea that by using a special technical vocabulary in a superstrict way and by arguing utterly rigorously philosophers can achieve an accurate transcription of the way things are out there, and definitive solutions to their classical problems. Instead, we need to acknowledge that philosophy does not and cannot jump completely clear of imaginative literature and myth, in the way it has traditionally pretended to do.

That is why, if you ask me what Being is, I can only reply that I am putting Being approximately where the ancient creation myths put talk of Chaos and the Primal Waters, the Deep. I am putting Being approximately where physicists nowadays put quantum fluctuations in the vacuum. There is no Absolute Being and no Absolute Nothingness. There are no hard straight lines, only wobbles: everywhere there is trembling, emergent contingency and statistical probabilities. So I am putting Being approximately where traditional philosophy put the whole realm of 'the possible'. So don't ask me whether or not the term Being corresponds to something out there. That's old thinking (or 'realism'). What you must do instead is look in a *literary* way at the job the word Being does – the contribution it makes to the picture I'm building. Remember, the picture I'm building is a sort of work of art. It is an art-picture of the way things are, and are with us humans. Philosophy (or at least, *edifying* philosophy) can't claim to be more than that.

As a work of art, a philosophy-book or a work of religious thought must seem very small-scale and amateurish when compared with the colossal and grandiose structures erected by modern natural science. But the scientists achieve their agreement and their results by limiting themselves to the questions that can be answered from a certain standpoint and by using certain agreed methods. They have problems with fitting themselves – their language, their consciousness, their knowledge, their values – smoothly into the world that they describe. And they have some problems with the status in the world and the destiny of the individual human being. Philosophy is left to tackle these questions that science either can't answer or sets aside. It paints a picture of the way things are, and are with us humans, that aims to be fully comprehensive, reflexively self-consistent, and usable in life by the single human individual. And because philosophical writing has to be highly reflexive, condensed and many-stranded, it has to be a kind of art.

All this is by way of explanation of the continuing influence of ancient creation myths in our thinking, and in this text. When we think about the relation between Being and Language we must find ourselves ruminating about darkness and light, about matter and form, about the primal waters and the Spirit moving above them, and about Chaos and Darkness jumping to attention when the all-powerful Word 'Let there be light' resounds over them.

So we say that Language moves over Being and calls it forth into beings, and so into becoming the world – that is, the lit-up human world, the *known* world, the world of Man. Heidegger, recalling in 1959 his earlier self of 1947, says:

Language was once called 'the House of Being'. It is the guardian of presencing, inasmuch as the latter's radiance remains entrusted to the propriative showing of the saying.[1]

That sounds dismal nonsense, but it seems to mean something that J. L. Austin would have recognized; namely, that spoken language is *declaratory* (it sheds light; *clarus* again), and *performative*.[2] It is a mode of action. It calls things up, shows things, points things out, *claims* things, establishes facts and builds a world. Our language builds the world of Man, which is the world as we know it; the world that is floodlit by our own conscious awareness of it, and of belonging to it.

I am talking anthropomonism again. I am equating Man with the world of Man, and the world of Man with the world, full stop. This point needs to be explained, and the explanation has to begin with the metaphor of *light*, which is very prominent both in Genesis and in Heidegger.

The world that language builds, the human world, the world of Man, is the clear (*clarus*) or known world, the world as it is in and for our human consciousness of it, the world described and illuminated precisely by the light of *consciousness*. Your consciousness may be defined as the lit-up-for-youness of the world of your present awareness. Accordingly, we should read the myth in *Genesis* as a myth about the origin of consciousness, which it correctly sees as co-eval with the beginnings in us of the motion of language. So you may read the Creation-myth in *Genesis* either as a myth about the origin of your own cosmology in your own earliest infancy, or as a myth about the origins of cosmology and consciousness in humanity generally. Language always brings with it both consciousness and a cosmology: that is how it works. Indeed, the two always belong together: if you are conscious, you have a world; and if you are a being that has a world, you are conscious. So when human beings first developed true language they began to acquire their first cosmology, and when you personally first heard and began to respond to language – perhaps even while you were still *your-self* in the primal, amniotic waters – *you* began to develop your own first cosmology. Language from the very first says this-and-not-that; it draws great lines across the Void, separating light from darkness, the self from the not-self, and so forth. The great distinctions both distinguish the self from the world, and divide up the world.

So the real world and the first world is the world described and theorized in language: not the world out there, allegedly independent of knowledge, but the world *in* our knowledge, the world formed by our language and lit up by our consciousness of it – in short, the everyday world we see. Far from the-world-in-our-knowledge being a secondary copy of the real world out there, the actual situation is the other way round. The world that is in your field of view and before your eyes just now – the life-world, the everyday world – is the world in knowledge. It is a world lit up by your own consciousness of it, by the ability to deploy the indexical pronouns through which we recognize the world as a *common* world, and still further lit up by your ability to describe and theorize everything in sight. You may be an antique dealer looking at a house interior, you may be a botanist looking at a hedgerow, you may be a houseproud person surrounded by family heirlooms and souvenirs, you may be a shopkeeper in your shop. The stories you'll wish to tell about the constituents of your world will vary according to your personal interests and history. But whatever be the case about that, you always have a highly-theorized world about you. You are conscious of space and time, of what everything is and its history. In short, the so-called 'real' world of the plain person is *not* the objective world that is said to be out there and inde-pendent of us, but the world in consciousness, the humanly-appropriated world. The first world is the world of experience, our world, the world of Man.

Now try to imagine the opposite, namely a world in which there is no conscious experience; a world that is purely objective because there is no being *for* whom it *is* a world. What's left? There might be electromagnetic vibrations, but there would be no colours, and presumably no *light* as such. There might be some sort of atmospheric vibrations, but no sound, no noise. There might be space and time, but there would be nobody who knows them as such. There might be occasional irregular collisions between complex systems, but there would be nothing that recognizes these systems as living bodies. In such a world, surely, there could be nothing more than physics in the dark – and perhaps not even that?

So you may say, 'Very well, I will give you consciousness and all the *qualia* or secondary qualities, and I will give you everything that depends upon our being the sort of organisms we are. But the mathematics would remain. The observerless world we are trying to imagine would still be a world that could be just as fully described in the language of mathematical physics as our own world is. And its mathematical description would be just as true of that world as the corresponding description would be of *our* world. This, let me tell you, is called by the philosophers of science "structural realism": it says that we'll grant you everything else, but at least the maths is out there. And from the numbers we might be able to make successful predictions about what the place might look like and feel like if a human astronaut with eyes and ears, a sense of space and time and balance, a scientific education and so on were by chance to arrive there. I accept that in the astronaut's absence all that is *there* is the actualized mathematical description. But when the astronaut arrives with human senses, a biological makeup, human consciousness and a scientific education that tells her or him what to expect – then, the flesh gets put on the bones and that world will become a *known* world, and a world *for* somebody just as ours is. The astronaut will be able to plant a flag and *claim* it.'

To which there is an obvious reply: 'In that far-off world, a few billion years ago or a few billion light years away, there is no mathematics, no language, and no representation. There is nobody and nothing that knows what it is for a mathematical representation to have application. We are talking about a world without any sort of knowledge or talk or consciousness, a world in total darkness. So we are not entitled to attribute even mathematical patterning to that world. It is nowhere, until somebody gets there.'

And do we not now begin to suspect that the world without consciousness, the world in the dark, the world before language, that we are trying to imagine is the world in Chaos and Darkness that the old creation-myths started from? They didn't start from absolute nothingness; they started from formless darkness and unconsciousness. In which case the creation myths are not myths about the first making of the sort of ready-made, fully-ordered but simply pre-human cosmos that popular scientific realism pictures, but myths about the first origin of *consciousness and the world-in-consciousness*, the human and lit-up sort of world I see and you see. The old myths recognize that the humanly-appropriated world is logically prior to the impersonal and objectified world portrayed by science. *Your* world is bigger than, and precedes, *the* world.

The most important point about the old creation myths – a point nobody ever makes – is the fact that they did not imagine, and could never have imagined, a lengthy period during which there was *a world without any beings for whom it was a world*. On the contrary, the world and human beings were portrayed as pretty much co-eval; and in any case there were always lots of gods and other spirits around for whom there was indeed a world. We were usually regarded as being indebted to them for the gift of language and for our consciousness of our world as world.

In fact, it is only since Darwin and the modern vast expansion of our cosmology that we have developed the notion of a world and maybe even a universe that exists fully formed for billions of years without there being anybody whose world it is; and even yet we have not fully grasped how queer and paradoxical a notion this is. Certainly it is a secondary and highly specialized development which comes after, and presupposes, the prior world-view that is built into ordinary language and everyday life. For that prior world-view the self and its world always belong – and develop – together. There is no entirely naked subject: to be a subject, I need a life, and therefore a world; and conversely, my life and my world need a subject to identify them as such. From infancy on it is obvious that to be a subject I must have a world in which I am situated; and to have a world I must be a subject, situated within it and with my own angle upon it. That is the primal situation: the first line of all divides light from darkness, and therewith the self from the not-self, its M/Other. The self, its world and its language *all develop together*.

That is why, in our representation here, we picture the (logical) primitives as Being, Language and Man. They all go all the way down, and Being is not any thing prior to Language. It is only the obscure, contingent forthcomingness, the uterine darkness that we seem always to presuppose but cannot clearly remember. It is the O, our M/Other. And we are always in a specific world, our world, the human world, the first world, our milieu and our 'objectivity'.

We picture Man, who is also the world of Man, as resulting from the interaction of language and Being. Heidegger is right to make a lot of the word *Eigen* or 'Own'. In English too there are complex and fascinating punning connections between own-ing and knowing. Knowing is linked with can (in the sense of 'knows how to'), kenning, canny, cunning and familiarization generally, and Owning is linked with self-possession (*on my own*), possession (*ownership*) and confession (*owning up*), as well as with the acknowledgement of kinship (in *owning*, as opposed to disowning, *a kinsman*). What we do not know is described as uncanny, uncouth, unkindly and unfamiliar. So Heidegger is right to say that language doesn't just describe the world and light it up as a scene or background against which to live our lives; more than that, through a range of complex linguistic acts we bind ourselves into our world, creating the various moral bonds through which we identify ourselves, and make our world our kn/own world. It is this own/known world of ours that is the primary world; and it emerges as the world of Man through the meeting of Being and Language in Man.

7. Man and Language

We are within spitting distance of the view that 'Man', Language and the world all concur and coincide, and differ only in being three different ways into one and the same entity or topic. For it is being suggested that 'Man' is the *animal symbolicum*, the creature that lives by symbolic expression and whose whole life has become a whirr of communicative activity. Around ourselves we build a picture-palace, a world of signs in motion. So Man is the human world, the human world is the world of signs, and since we are always inside our picture-palace, our cultural world of dancing signs is for us effectively *the* world absolutely. In our own media age the most thoroughgoing form of postmodern philosophy, namely the philosophy of the sign, treats all reality as a process of signs. Its aim is to eliminate ontology, the traditional theory of being. Meaning, reference and truth are all treated simply in terms of the relations between signs, and no appeal is made to any metasignitive 'reality' whatever.

Here, I am not taking quite such a strict view. Instead I am working around a triad of interdependent themes or 'principles': Being, Man and Language. None of the three is fixed: they can all be moved around a bit. The reason for this is that we are concerned here with edifying philosophy – with religion and the question of happiness – which means that I need to open some spaces, between Man and Being, between the self and other selves, and even between Man and Language. In these spaces one can poetize religious relationships: in the space between Man and Being one can write (as we have done, and will do) the difference between the Fear of Being and the Love of Being; in the space between the self and other selves one can write the difference between the religious desire to lose oneself and the religious desire for the self's social fulfilment in communion with others; and in the space between Man and Language one can write the difference between Language and silence, between the affirmation and the negation of images, and between the sense in which we make Language and the sense in which Language makes and gives itself to us.

By introducing the terms of art Being, Man and Language, I am not returning to metaphysics. None of the three is a substance, and none is foundational or irreducible. The purpose of the move is simply to get religious writing going. Since religious writing is the most potent and happiness-producing kind of writing that there is, a new lease of life for religious writing will make everything better. It will add zip to the motion of the entire world of signs. It will not postulate any substances, but it will get everything moving.

We have already claimed that, although they are co-extensive and deeply interfused, the human world and the world of language – that is, Man and Language – should not be simply identified. It is well worth distinguishing them, and opening a little space between them, because as we do so we perceive the manifold religious character of our own relation to language. Language gives us the symbolic forms in which we can express ourselves and become ourselves: it draws us out into public and coherent expression, and thereby integrates us. The socially-presented self that goes on show and negotiates with others is the cultural self-objectification in and through which we become persons. Our true feelings are still readable, but they are represented in a symbolic guise that decently veils as well as reveals them. Conflicting feelings – as when, for example, we are both attracted to and wary of someone else – are thus turned into social courtesies and so made manageable and inoffensive.

Language produces the relatively-integrated, presentable, social human self; but more than that, we also experience the relation to Language as thoroughly religious just within subjectivity. Language is experienced as the *currency* of thought; that is, it supplies not only the code, but also its endlessly-running (literally, 'current') character. Thoughts are words, and they run in trains. When we sit down to write a letter, we wait for *inspiration*; we wait for language to come running, giving us the words we are waiting for. They just pop up; they *come to mind*. Come to mind: thinking is a receptive waiting-upon Language. We experience Language as a pervasive life-giving, formative and world-building power:[1] as being, in fact, just what the old language of religion used to call 'the Spirit'. And in our tradition we have always been quite at ease with the overlap between the supposedly-secular notion of being poetically inspired by language and the strictly supernatural notion of divine inspiration by the motion of the Holy Spirit.

The relation to Language is religious all-through. Language is like spirit. I feel it every day now, running through me, making me, energizing me, expressing itself in and *as* me, revealing my troubled and divided make-up but also working to heal and integrate me. Should one speak of Language as the medium in and through which we live and enact the relation to Being? Maybe, but there are also those times when one meditates, slowing down and down until as Language stops we just for an instant seem to sense pure Being. So the relation to the motion of Language is religious, and so also is the relation to the cessation of Language.

And we find that the religious relation is *always* now a relation in which the *relata* are neither numerically two nor numerically one. The best analogy for this is perhaps the relation of the artwork to the artist. The work we are making is our own self-expression and self-objectification, which we own as our own even as we put it out. So the three relations, between Being and Man, between Being and Language, and between

Man and Language, are all of them relations between objects that are neither numerically two nor simply numerically one. The Fountain – the beginningless, endless, purely-contingent flow of everything – is three in one, and one in three.

The trinitarian analogy can be developed a little further. When we concentrate attention upon Being and the continual coming-forth of the world *ex nihilo*, we seem to be reinstating metaphysics. When we concentrate attention upon Man, we seem to be picturing humans as themselves the makers of all meanings and all truths; the makers of all they know and own. And when we concentrate attention upon Language, we seem to see everything – including ourselves and our world – as produced within and by the dance of signs. If we write Being as the generative principle and source of everything, we seem to be reviving some form of Realism. It we write Man as the first principle, and picture everything as being shaped within and by human consciousness, we seem to be reviving Idealism. And if we write the motion of Language as generating everything, somewhat as a cine-projector makes a world on a screen out of a flickering play of light, we seem to be talking some form of postmodernism or semiotics. 'What is going on here?', says a critical friend, feeling that my text is pulling in different ways. He thinks I'm being inconsistent.

In reply, I am not mapping a real Truth of things, out there. There is no such thing, and the very idea of a coherent totalizing system of dogmatic belief, whether metaphysical or theological, is dead. What we are doing here is something very different. Consider the way the Trinity presents three different possible foci of religious attention. One may focus on God as transcendent unifying Centre and source of all authority and legitimation, or as the object of abstract contemplation; one may, by concentrating attention upon the Son, see the divine in human, social and ethical terms; and one may, by foregrounding the Spirit, attend to the utopian, charismatic and even disruptive face of religion. The divine has several faces – coeternally and coequally as we are assured – and one may (poetically) believe in their unity; but one cannot *argue* it, in detail.

Similarly, in our secularized and immanentized version of trinitarian thinking, we will find that our world-view has several faces – realistic, radical-humanist, and semiotic, for example. If one can write them into a poetical sort of unity, that's fine and perhaps even felicific: but old-style systematic unity? No: that is gone, and we should give up nostalgia for it. I am trying to suggest that if we give up nostalgia for the old certainties, we may still be able to experience religious happiness, even in a world that has become flowing, temporal, secondary and deconstructed, all the way down.

8. The Contingency of Being, Man and Language

In the Western tradition as it developed after Plato, there was for a very long period a striking degree of agreement amongst philosophers and religious thinkers about the Supreme Good and highest object of human aspiration. The chief end (*finis ultimus*) of human life was a state of absolute knowledge by intellectual intuition of an absolute object. In religion this object was called simply God. In philosophy it also had other names, such as the Good, the One, God or Nature (*Deus sive Natura*), and the Absolute; but there was widespread agreement about how to characterize it. It was One, supremely Real, eternal, perfect, infinite and necessarily-existent.

Knowledge of this object was usually not innate in human beings, but had to be acquired by an arduous discipline. In assisting the progress of the soul towards its supreme good and last end, the philosophers laid the most emphasis on rigorous intellectual training and the clarification of the understanding, whereas the theologians spoke more about moral purification and the illumination of the mind by God's Spirit. Both parties tended to see the supreme Good as fully attained only after or in death, but they both allowed that the philosopher or the saint might enjoy an anticipatory taste of it in this present life.

Human life was thus seen as a great journey through time towards eternity, in which one hoped at last to enter a consummating state of absolute knowledge of something that was at once supremely Real and perfectly Good. In this knowledge

– the Vision of God, as religion called it – one would enjoy eternal happiness.

In retrospect, we might now be inclined to ask: *Why?* If God or the One was infinite and simple, 'without body, parts, or passions', why should the timeless contemplation of God constitute a human being's highest happiness? Imagine looking into a completely empty sky; imagine contemplating the mathematical infinite; imagine looking for ever at a mathematical proof; imagine being without senses or feelings. Is this sort of thing a human being's highest good? The Isle of Wight is notorious as a place whose denizens can be relied upon to campaign bitterly against the threat of even the smallest change ever taking place; but one doubts whether even *they* really and in their heart of hearts truly desire eventless eternity. And is there not in any case a paradox about desiring the eternal cessation of desire?

Why then did the great religious and philosophical traditions of the Near East and India come to be dominated by the idea that a human being is a creature so constituted that it cannot be fully happy in this world, and must instead spend all its life in preparation for a bodiless, timeless world of intellectual contemplation to be entered after death? Part of the answer lies in the fact that the early Iron Age was a time of great world-pessimism and warring city-states, in which men were often led to destruction by the violence of their passions. Life for most people was laborious and wretched beyond our present imagining. And it was also an age of genius in which people were becoming intensely excited by the invention of mathematics, logic, theory, education and the first organized bodies of secular knowledge. A new type of human being, the disciplined intellectual, the researcher, the thinker, the philosopher, was appearing. To his contemporaries this character seemed like a 'divine man', a *theios aner*. People like him should rule the state, or at least be the advisors of kings. How could lesser people come to share his virtues?

The Revelation of Being

Against this background, some at least of what we call the great 'world religions' developed as democratizations of philosophy and the moral training associated with it – Christianity and Buddhism being the most obvious examples.[1] Jesus and the Buddha were at first perceived and portrayed by the world beyond their own immediate circle as having been philosophers, the early teachers of the faith dressed and behaved like itinerant philosophers, and theological writers could claim that the new teaching was 'the one true philosophy'. The account of St Paul at Athens in the Acts of the Apostles indicates that the presentation of the new faith as a philosophy goes back to very early times.

Paul's own ethical teachings, along with those of other early Christian and Buddhist writers, are indebted to the philosophical tradition, and teach the traditional virtues of the counsellor and the wise man: temperance, tolerance, and a mild conciliatory spirit of impartial benevolence. One should be peaceable, moderate, sober and law-abiding, forgiving and generous.

In modern culture we tend to assume that religion and philosophy are very different from each other, and to see religion as being either non-rational or supra-rational. We tend to forget the extent to which both Christianity and Buddhism were originally spread, perceived, admired and received as philosophies. The character-type 'the monk' is historically descended from another traditionally-celibate figure, the philosopher of antiquity: the monk's habit was once the philosopher's cloak.

Against this background one can see popular religious belief, with its orientation towards self-control, resignation, the long view, contemplative values and the eternal world as functioning to help ordinary people to take life *philosophically* – the term being much more accurate than is usually recognized. In an age when life was very harsh and laborious, one can see why people longed for the everlasting rest of the saints; in times when one could be destroyed by the sudden and reckless violence of the passions, people understandably took to a discipline that promised deliverance from them; and when *a priori* reasoning of any kind was a rather recent invention one can understand that the intellectual satisfaction it gives might be taken as an image of eternal happiness.

So for a long period the disciplines of other-worldly religion did successfully bring something of the consolations of philosophy to people in general. But that was then: this is now. It occurs to me that the revelation of being which occurred in July 1997 was in many ways significant precisely as a reversal of the older values. We live in a technological-bureaucratic world, dominated by means-end rationality, theory and long-termism. We are habitually so long-termist, planning our careers, mortgages and pensions in terms of decades, that our life threatens to lose its savour. In that context, the old Platonic valuations and disciplines have become unattractive. We don't want any *more* long-termism: we've got too much of that already. Instead, we might look to religion to help us return into sensuous immediacy and the affirmation of intrinsic value in the here and now. The revelation of being was therefore *not* purely intellectual; on the contrary, it took place in the visual field, eyes open. One was enraptured, not by eternity, but by surfing pure temporality; and one delighted not in necessity of being but in the gratuitous happenstance just of contingency, the way it all just happens to be turning out. No reason: it's fine, just as it is. No reason: pure delight.

Let us recapitulate. It was a sunny day: I looked out southward from an upper window over the 300-metre grassy square (or rhombus) of Parker's Piece. Grass fluoresces a little in sunshine, so that the broad acreage of green throbbed at one with vegetable vitality. It was as usual liberally sprinkled with people, dogs, kites, bicycles, gulls, pushchairs, and footballs moving back and forth. Around the edges of the big common trees swayed, and motor traffic crawled and stopped, crawled and stopped. Above, clouds were changing shape as they surged across a broad East Anglian sky. Sitting very still and watching,

I saw the purely-contingent moment-by-moment forthcoming of Be-ing. I saw Language running everywhere across the scene, forming everything, describing everything, making everything intelligible, appropriating everything into Man, the human world, the *field*. And perhaps it was the pun on 'field' that threw me: the field of view, the field of our shared public consciousness, this grassy field in the sunshine. Let it be; it's all one to me.

All *One*? In the revelation of being everything is seen to be contingent. It just happens to be the way it is. We cannot claim that it-all is in some hidden way unified, either by threads of logically-necessary connection linking the different elements of the scene, or by their all being grounded in a metaphysical Substance. We are not talking about any form of determinism or pantheism. We no longer expect everything to come together at the end of history. Yet the impulse to invoke the idea of unity remains. Why? I think it lies in our sudden realization of the three-way fit, the outsideless for-each-otherness, of Being, Man and Language. A difficult and novel idea – but it is what we are pursuing.

All one *to me*? Notice, and set aside for consideration later, the way I felt drawn out into the field. In science, the self remains an ideal observer, detached and distinct from the observer. But in religion and art, the self takes pleasure in giving up its own distinctness and pouring itself out into, or yielding itself up to, the other.

9. The Temporality of Being, Man and Language

Time in mythology is an ambivalent figure, sometimes female, sometimes male. An old Chinese saying pictures Time as a 'dark woman' whose body gives birth to everything, and then in due course becomes everything's grave. In the West time is very ancient, and male. He, Chronos, is both the Father of Zeus and the castrator of his own father Ouranos, the sky or heaven.

Time is dark and dual, a creator and a destroyer. On the one hand, it is the condition of the possibility of everything: all be-ing, all language and everything human are alike both subject to and dependent upon temporal succession. Time is the condition for the delivery of linguistic meaning (which always arrives somewhat belatedly), and therewith Time is also the condition for consciousness (which also arrives in arrears), and for Truth. Everything comes to be *piecemeal*, successively, a bit at a time. (Hence perhaps the myth of time as a castrator: it salami-slices everything. Ouch.)

So there is no non-temporal Being. Everything comes to be, and is apprehended or understood bit by bit, in time. But Time, which delivers – or is delivered of – everything, also puts an end to everything. Everything is be(com)ing, everything is subject to changes and chances, and everything – truths and values, particles and galaxies – has a finite life-span. Just the wear and tear of time and chance produces everything and then eventually erodes everything away. Everything is on the skids, and nothing is wholly and securely self-present; therefore there are no substances.

The Revelation of Being

We haven't been too keen to recognize this. Consider, for example, how long philosophers in the West contrived to cling on to the ideas both of *substance* and of *causality*, without admitting how deeply they are at odds with each other. We held on to the idea of substance, because it gives us a way of saying that some important objects, such as human souls, are independent and indestructible beings that can maintain their identity unaffected by the passage of time. But this notion of a simple immortal substance is incompatible with the notion of genuine causal interaction between beings. If I am subject to change, then I do *not* remain indestructibly self-identical. A causal influence that acts upon me, *changes* me. Indeed nothing remains for ever unchanged. Because everything is secondary and everything is interwoven, everything surges and heaves and changes together.[1] For example, in the 1960s I was a bit of 'the Sixties', and in the 1990s I am a bit of 'the Nineties', and I now differ at least as much from myself-then as the Nineties differ from the Sixties. The human self is of course historically-situated, and there is no way it can *not* be interwoven with the evolving cultural world of which it is part. Our world is our own objectivity, and as such is part of us: we make it, it makes us.

In reply you may wish to point out the innumerable ways in which culture promises immortality, or at least remembrance, to us. Symbolically, at least, we try to create monuments that bear our name and stand forth as public tokens of our continuing identity. A register, a record, a roll of honour, a list, a certificate, an inscription, a child, a book, a signed work, a building, a business, a 'lifetime achievement award', a named scholarship, and even simply a fixed abode or last home – the sheer number and variety of these devices bears eloquent testimony to their futility: if even *one* of them really worked, it would be enough. But in fact the rather desperate manner in which the elderly grasp at any available tokens of present public recognition and future remembrance betrays their knowledge that they will soon be forgotten, along with everyone and everything else. Nothing whatever guarantees or can guarantee the eternal conservation of Reason itself, or of any meaning, or truth, or value, or of the identity of a person or anything else. Some philosophers whom I have known began in their last years to dream of a cosmic memory-bank or data-base in which everything is stored up forever.[2] They seem to have persuaded themselves that they could derive some real consolation from this idea. But they deceived themselves, for nothing guarantees the eternal conservation of anything. All is becoming, and all beings, meanings, truths and values have a finite lifespan.

The effect of these considerations is to put an end to the future as something that we might appeal to in order to make up for the deficiencies of the present. The future is a broken reed, and we should not be surprised to find that the two great cultures that have been preoccupied with thoughts of an immensely long cosmic timescale, namely classical India and the modern West, have both been troubled by pessimism. But now, everything returns into the present. We can't look to another and distant era for justification. We and everything we cherish are intimately bound up with the way things are now, in such a way that we cannot even begin to imagine how the whole frame of things could be altered so as to immortalize all the things we cherish, whilst yet keeping them the same as they are now and are dear to us. How could there be life, or meaning, or selfhood, or delight, except *in time*; and how could you be what you are, my dear, except in this particular period in which we are living? We must give up vainly imagining an Elsewhere, and start being solar *here*. We must say Yes to life, not if and when, but Now.

There is only *all this*; all this is all there is. And the Revelation of Being is a paradoxical revelation of the way be-ing and language and humanity are all interwoven in a totality that is all the way through only finite and contingent and temporal. Yet it is enough for us, and we see that it is profitless to try to imagine how things might be otherwise. If the ideas of 'salvation' and 'eternal life' still have any meaning, it has to be found and affirmed simply in the contingent Now. When we learn solar living we say yes to things as they are.[3] What we've got is enough. It is 'our objectivity'; it is all ours, and it is enough. It is all there could be, and all that we could be consistently asking for.

And here a most remarkable shift has taken place. In the older philosophies and in classical theism one found final intellectual satisfaction and happiness in the vision of something that was eternal and perfect, and logically *had* to be what it was. One was taken up into the Infinite. The human spirit could not finally be content with anything less than eternal necessity and absolute perfection of being. So it was from Parmenides to Hegel. But now I am saying that we can and must find the same eternal happiness here and now, and in the vision of everything as being only contingent, only finite, only temporal and 'perishing' and outsideless. Heidegger's three-in-one-and-one-in-three Trinity of Being, Man and Language is an extraordinary secularization, enhistorization, finitization of the Christian Triune God; but to be born of it, part of it, and live and die in it can give us the same happiness. For what we are here describing is a postmodern, temporalized and deconstructed version of the traditional Vision of God, a secular theology.

10. The Outsidelessness of Being, Man and Language

In philosophy, at least, we should avoid talking about 'the Universe', because there is nothing to assure us that there is a ready-made, intelligible and coherent order of things out there. We have no way of knowing that a great line or boundary is drawn around everything to wrap it up and bind it together like a haggis, so as to make of it just one big Thing, however heterogeneous and repellent. There is no whole System of things out there and independent of us. *We* do all the system-building. Nothing says that there is just one great Truth of all things, or just one way that things have to be and are. So it is important that we should understand that Being, Man and Language do not comprise a Totality, like Spinoza's God-or-Nature or like the Absolute in Idealist philosophy. There is no Totality. Instead, one should think of Being, Man and Language simply as three different gateways into philosophy, each with its own angle, style, approach, vocabulary. When we think of Being, we think of the continual temporal forthcoming of everything; when we think of Man, we think of the way everything gets named, claimed and appropriated into the human world; and when we think of Language, we think of the whole humming world of symbolic exchange that draws Being forth into beings and fills the world of Man.

By using imagery of breath, wind and vibration, we suggest that everything may be seen as (sort-of) living. So at least I saw it, in July 1997. Every thing is as it were 'organically' interconnected, in Man, by Language. Every thing is gratuitous, temporal, interwoven, secondary, incomplete and historically-developing. But we are always *in medias res*, in the middle of things. We never find an *arché* (a foundation, First Principle or absolute Beginning) of all things, and we never find the *telos* (or Last End) of all things. It is this contingency and temporality of every thing that prevents us from attaining to any final systematization of things. Which is just as well. As things are, it is as if everything is metaphorically alive and growing. But if everything were to slot into its final position and come to rest, so that motion and time and Language were all to stop as well, everything would metaphorically die. For there to be life or consciousness, there has to be time and change and finitude. So we should be happy to be always on the go, and in the midst of it all. There is nowhere else to be.

In the past I have called this view of everything 'energetic Spinozism'. But it is markedly different from Spinozism, in that when motion, contingency and temporality are brought to the fore we preclude any sort of 'theological' totalization of everything. Every thing and everything has slipped away a bit before it has ever completely arrived.

In which case, you may well retort, why am I chuntering through a string of short chapters that assign to Being, Man and Language a series of attributes that appear to be modelled upon the traditional metaphysical attributes of God?

The answer is that I am pointing up a contrast between the traditional *transcendent* metaphysical attributes of God and the *transcendental* conditions to which in modern philosophy everything is seen as being subject. Thus, instead of the Divine Eternity we speak of everything's being *temporal*; instead of the Divine Necessity we speak of everything's being *contingent*; and instead of the Divine Infinity we speak of everything's being *outsideless*, and so on.

In the past there was very commonly thought to be a deductive, and indeed an analytic, connection between the various infinite metaphysical attributes of God. In the Divine Simplicity they all simply coincided, so that it seemed obvious that one could argue that if God is p, then he must also be q, and r, and s and so on. Accordingly Anselm of Canterbury argues that God is by definition the greatest conceivable Being, who is everything that it is better to be than not to be; and that therefore God must exist, must exist of and through himself alone, must have all metaphysical and moral perfections, must be the Creator of all that is not himself, and so forth.[1]

This relatively-tight and deductive interconnection of the Divine attributes evidently depends historically upon certain deep assumptions that go back to Plato. In particular, Plato believes that the Supreme Good must be also the Supremely Real and the most Intelligible; and he believes in the unity of all the virtues in the Good. In the subsequent tradition it was very commonly thought evident that all metaphysical and moral perfections must coincide and be identical in the Divine Essence; so that obviously one *could* argue analytically that they must all entail each other, round in a circle.

Modern post-metaphysical philosophy rejects Plato's framework, claiming to know only one world, namely this world, and only one sort of being, namely timebound finite being. In Hobbes' version, the general transcendental condition governing all finite being is *motion* or change: in Heidegger's twentieth-century version of the new doctrine, the general transcendental condition governing all finite be-ing is temporality. We reject the metaphysical idea of eternal Being and its infinite attributes and confine ourselves to the world we know, the human world, the world of Becoming, the world of finite, human-type, historically *situated* be-ing, *Dasein*.

Now Heidegger is nothing if not a theologian – by which I mean that like most of the German philosophers since Hegel he is deeply influenced by Latin Christian, and especially Lutheran, thought, and his whole vision of the human condition is a sort of secularization of Lutheran theology. So can he argue around a circle of inter-related transcendental conditions of *Dasein*, much as the old dogmatic theology had argued around a circle of transcendent metaphysical attributes of God?

No: he cannot. The connections are not going to be deductive or analytic, because we have given up that sort of philosophy. But at least Heidegger can and does start with temporality, and on that point he's right. We can and we must repudiate the notions of timeless Being, timeless life, timeless intelligence, timeless utterance and so on. We've got to start thinking of all being as temporally conditioned, as Be(com)ing. In these moving sentences, in your perusal of them, and in the motion of the world about you. And if be-ing is always becoming, we should give up the old mythic impulse to picture temporal Becoming as having long ago issued from eternal Being, and as one day returning into it. We should give up all talk of absolute beginnings and last ends. We didn't originate somewhere else, and we are not going to end up in some other place. We are always and *outsidelessly* here, *in via*, on the way, in process. So everything is always subject to time and chance, temporality and contingency.

By talking of 'outsidelessness', I mean that we should learn to give up the old habit of seeking to explain, or evaluate, or justify the way things are now by reference to some greater and better order of things elsewhere – whether up above, or in the beginning, or yet to come. We can, we do and we must care about democratic politics, about art, and about our values, without ever again falling into the old error of supposing that our commitments in these areas need to be grounded in some past Golden Age when all the rules were laid down; or that our commitments need to be justified by reference to some standard-setting higher order of things, or by reference to a state of final perfection that will one day be reached. Everything has got to be understood to make sense and be worthwhile just now, and on its own terms; and that goes for art *of course*, and for democratic politics, for our values, and for language itself, and (I insist) also for religion. Everything must be understood to make sense immanently and currently. Meaning itself is immanent and current.

Notice here a pleasant and instructive ambiguity in the word *currency*. From *currere*, to run, it means the state of being current, in circulation, moving around in the public realm. But the word *currency* signifies more than just being in motion and being actively traded; it also means *having a certain clear meaning or value, that is given by the terms upon which it is being daily exchanged*. In which case its currency in certain exchanges *is* its meaning, in the case of a word; or its value, in the case of a commodity. Its currency is its current rating or valuation.

This is fascinating, and radically anti-Platonic. In Platonism, motion and change are always associated with corruption and decay. The 'valuables' in which you stored your wealth were relatively-incorruptible objects that you kept safely locked away – *out of circulation*, as the phrase goes. Heaven itself was pictured as a sort of bank vault, where nothing bad can happen to your treasures.

Nevertheless, human life involves a great deal of exchange. How was the value of the tokens that are constantly traded back and forth to be maintained? The old answer was to link them to fixed and unchanging standards, supposedly exalted above the flux. The gold standard in finance; the 'real' and founding meanings of words, as given by their etymologies; absolute moral values and commandments, as vested in our traditions and religious institutions.

But during the nineteenth century a big change took place. Gradually, people gave up the idea that *currency erodes value* unless its tokens are anchored to timeless and unchangeable standards of value, and instead they began to accustom themselves to the new idea that *currency establishes value*. The social market *is* the Last Judgement! We may disagree with the current verdict of the market, and seek to change it. But we cannot any longer make the old metaphysical distinction between the current consensus of the market about a thing's value, and its real, eternal value by some transcendent standard. We have no access to any such transcendent or 'absolute' standards. If we feel that a particular painter is overrated or a particular poet is underrated, then we must enter the fray with our own arguments for a change in the current valuation. And that's all.

Now you see what I mean by outsidelessness. I mean radical immanence. People hate it. They think up abusive names for it: it is capitalism, it is materialism, it is 'trendy' liberalism, it is nihilism, it represents the end of all real and abiding values. The confused tirade of abuse that people direct against it reveals their crippling fear of Being.[2]

But the Revelation of Being is a vision of things – of Being, Man and Language – as humming, brimming, glowing with life and value. Everything is immanent, transactional, secondary – and yet, extraordinarily *radiant*. Hence the idea of *solar living*, and of a religious life that is entirely content with all this, just this, outsidelessly.

11. The Coextensiveness of Being, Man and Language

Let us repeat: by 'Man' we mean simply the human world, the realm across which language runs to and fro, the world of consciousness, the lit-up world *of* which we are aware and *in* which we all of us participate. By 'Man' I mean just the world you're in, and the form of consciousness you've already got. Beautiful idioms call it 'broad daylight', or 'the light of common day'. It is maintained as our public and common world just by the motion of language. Words are general, and their constant circulation keeps them meaningful. They are common currency, and the fact that the same forms of words, spinning around, run through me and also through you and others too makes us all communicant members in an illuminated communal world, the world of Man.

I'm made of and by the torrent of words that runs through me each day, and you are made of and by the torrent of words that runs through you. The very considerable linguistic overlap between us all ensures that there is and there has to be an equally considerable overlap of consciousness or subjectivity between people. It is sometimes suggested that different individuals may perhaps associate entirely different subjective 'feels' or *qualia* with the same words – colour-words, for example; and it is also sometimes suggested that the subjective experience of male persons is quite different from that of female persons. This cannot be so, because subjective consciousness is created by the motion of the common language, which is exactly the same for women as for men, and must therefore conjure up the very same 'interior' and subjective illumination.

You may reply that when a man and a woman read the same novel, perhaps the man as he reads identifies with the hero and the woman as she reads identifies with the heroine. Both peruse the same stream of text; but they position themselves differently as they read, and to that extent they may have different experiences and seem to read different texts. To which the obvious retort is that in reading a novel or seeing a movie we all of us have no difficulty in identifying trans-sexually, and often *must* do so, because of the way the work we are following has been constructed. In fact, members of each sex take pleasure in identifying with someone of the other. So we should give up the fancy, or the jocular pretence, that there is something mysterious and systematically hidden from us in the subjectivity of any person of the opposite sex. On the contrary, it's all in the language, and nothing is hidden. Everything that a woman is, is already given in the language, and everything that a man is, is already given in the language. There is no mystery, either in sex or in religion, and there are *not* more things in heaven and earth than are dreamt of in my philosophy. What is religious about life is not that it is mysterious, but on the contrary, that it is so *un*mysterious, such a gift, so broad and plain. Now, *that* is wonderful. The worlds of Man and of Language are in the minutest detail reciprocally-adapted and coextensive. They couldn't be a more perfect fit than they are. Nor is this surprising: they have evolved and are still evolving to fit each other.

I am saying that the worlds of Man and Language are coextensive; but I am not saying that the ring-fence around the one is the same ring-fence as the ring-fence around the other. There is no fence. We should do without any talk of an encircling limit, ring-fence or boundary running around either 'thought', or language, or our world. In the Preface to the *Tractatus*, Wittgenstein tells us that the book will draw a limit to thinking, the old Kantian ambition. The idea is to have a *cordon sanitaire* separating sense from nonsense. But Wittgenstein himself recognizes even as he states it that the very project of drawing a line around the edges of language is reflexively paradoxical:

> . . . in order to draw a limit to thinking we should have to be able to think both sides of this limit (we should therefore have to be able to think what cannot be thought).
>
> The limit can, therefore, only be drawn in language and what lies on the other side of the limit will be simply nonsense.[1]

But even that will not do. It still makes the mistake of picturing what is unintelligible as occupying *a further stretch* of mappable territory that begins on the far side of the boundary fence that encircles meaningful discourse. Which is absurd. Non-sense is a non-place. It would be much better and less misleading to picture the world of Language as finite but unbounded, like the Universe in modern physical cosmology. We never arrive at its edge and we do not enlarge it by pushing back any boundary fence. Like the world of the cosmologists, the world of language simply *expands*, pushing out and creating new territory by internal differentiation, by the development of new regions of discourse and by the growth of knowledge. The great enrichment since the eighteenth century of our vocabulary for talking about human psychology is an excellent example. Developing new metaphors and new ways of talking about the self, writers like William James and Freud expanded a certain region of discourse, and thereby opened up new vistas, new territory.

So the motion of language opens up, differentiates and illuminates – that is, makes clear, conscious and intelligible – the whole world of Man, both on its objective side (the common world) and on its subjective side (the self). Both Language and Man are finite, but unbounded and outsideless. They expand by their own internal differentiation, as poets and other creative people make new metaphors and enrich the language.

The Revelation of Being

The way Language and Man are coextensive and evolve together is neatly illustrated by the way Freud not only enriched the language by giving us a lot of new vocabulary for talking about psychology, but he also thereby heightened our self-awareness and enhanced our ability to read each other's behaviour. The coining of new metaphors, the enrichment of the language, the growth of knowledge, and the making of a bigger and more brightly-lit human world are all part of the same process. (And, by the way, all this stands despite the extent to which Freud just at the moment is wildly unfashionable.)

But now the question of the coextensiveness of Being with Man and Language arises, and is trickier because the terms in which I've just been describing the growth of the worlds of language and of man seem to suggest that the whole doctrine of Being may be redundant. Does it do any useful work? Why not simply leave it out, and be content instead to explain everything in terms simply of the philosophy of language?

To take the question of 'Man' first, I want there to be 'Man' because I want there to be *consciousness-of* and *understanding*. I don't want Language to be all there is. It is a tool, so there need to be tool-users. And if the world is a communications network then we need to describe the terminals that are receiving and broadcasting messages, and we need to say how the flux of communication gives rise to our common, brightly-lit, consciously-experienced, public human world. I agree with those anti-Cartesians who say that *self*-consciousness is not of the very first importance. But consciousness-*of*, in the sense of participation in a clearly-perceived-and-collectively-understood common human world, is of the first importance. It is what I'm calling Man with a capital letter, the concrete universal, the *Humanum*. The peculiarity of us human beings is that we are not just, like other beings, constituents of a world, but that we ourselves *have* a world which we are aware of and that we have built. I'm putting this human world of ours first, and correlating

72

it with ordinary language. Philosophically, we need to get clear about *it* first, and *then* we can recognize that the great scientific narratives of cosmic, biological and human evolution are useful secondary constructions, *within* it.

Fair enough: we need Language, and we need Man, in order to gain a basic philosophical understanding of how it is that we can be what we are, communicate as we do, and have the common human world that we have. *But do we need Being?* Suppose we start by explaining Being as follows: 'The being of a thing is the difference that remains between even the fullest possible description of it, and the thing itself. In short, Being is non-language. ~~Being~~ is the extra-linguistic stuff out there that our descriptive uses of language are trying to refer to, or be about. Being is only-contingent, and it is slipping-away all the time. Sometimes I think of it as supporting our descriptive utterance rather as a rising jet of hot air supports a hot-air balloon. But ~~Being~~ is non-language: that is to say, that since it is by definition the one and only thing that can't be captured in language (for it is always presupposed by, prior to and outside language), we cannot describe it. Many unphilosophical people – if I understand them – seem to hold that the thing out-there in reality exists as an exact replica of its description in language. Naive realism, that is, seems to be saying that brown cows going on being just straightforwardly brown cows even after the *words* "brown cows" have been taken away. But that doesn't make sense. Try again; but this time *really* take the words away. What is the truly extra-linguistic and wordless thing? Since we are ourselves always in language, we can't actually *say*. Because we think only in language, we cannot quite think Being. We can sort-of attend to it, have an attitude to it, and respond to it, but it is inevitably lost in the course of any attempt to take it into the world of language.' Now, when you've taken in all this I suspect you are going to come over all British and philistine. You're going to say: 'Instead of going on and on about why Being can't be talked about, wouldn't it be better and more economical just to SHUT UP? Why not save your breath and simply leave out Being?'

In reply to this expostulation, I am *not* going to say that we need there to be a real extra-linguistic order of things out there to act as a touchstone against which to check the truth of indicative statements. There is no such thing as the act of matching-up a sentence against a solid, shapely, extra-linguistic fact. So far as truth is concerned, we can give a satisfactory account of it simply in terms of what I have been calling Man and Language. We need refer only to ways of speaking, beliefs and usages that are current, make sense, do a useful job, help us to get around and get things done, and so on.

But I *do* want Being for what may be called ethical and religious reasons. It is our needed complementary Other. It slows us down, stabilizes us, settles and situates us. It represents to us, and indeed it *is*, our life's pure abyssal transience, which sometimes makes me sick with metaphysical horror but at other times moves me to intense love. It makes me feel *solar*. And when we think about our life's purely gratuitous gift of itself to us, and of Being as the religious object, and about everybody's need to find their own Way from the Fear of Being to the Love of Being, the question arises of the special relationship between Man and Being.

A scientist might put the point by reflecting in wonderment that Man is the animal in whom the Universe has at last become conscious of itself. In us the Universe is suddenly illuminated; it has turned around and begun to theorize itself and explore itself. That is a wonderful thing. Put it in a language closer to Heidegger's, and we may say: 'Other beings are constituents of a world, but the human being is the being that is so sociable and communicative that is *has* a world. We've built our world in and through our own furiously-energetic networking, which has made us both conscious of our common world and individually self-conscious; but more than that, we are the beings who have been galvanized by the Question of Being. Just our awed recognition of the extreme lightness and emptiness of Being is what has driven us to invent religions, build systems of knowledge and create works of art.' In short, the special relationship between Man and Being has made us what we are, and is still the motor that drives us.

There are no substances, and no eternal truths. Everything is transient, flitting away so fast that as soon as it's come it is already going. And this gives us the context in which to set the maxim, 'Man is Being's poem'. By that I mean that in the human world, in human consciousness, and especially in our human consciousness of transience and being-towards-death, Being achieves its completest expression. We say Yes to Being when we accept our own finitude and mortality.

An interesting corollary, rarely spelled out, is that we should consciously renounce life after death and not merely remain half-hopefully agnostic about it. Nietzsche says somewhere that so long as human beings were passionately concerned with the next world, they didn't have the motivation to commit themselves to any great projects in this one. To quote the local Cambridge illustration, the Romans made a start on draining the Fens, but during the Christian period nothing was done, and the work was resumed only in the seventeenth century. Only if you are acutely conscious of time and death can you develop an historical sense, and begin to envisage really large-scale and this-worldly projects and calculations.

The essential insight here can unite philosophers who are otherwise more-or-less wholly at Loggerheads.[2] Bernard Williams, in 'The Makropulos case: reflections on the tedium of immortality',[3] decides that 'an endless life would be a meaningless one', and gives all the right reasons. He quotes Aristotle's splendid saying about Plato's form of the Good to the effect that it is not 'any the more good for being eternal: that which lasts long is no whiter than that which perishes in a day' (Nicomachean Ethics, 1096^b 4). What is precious is no more precious for being eternal, and, conversely, no less so for being transient. And in saying all this, Williams is unexpectedly close to Heidegger – a philosopher of whom he has a very low opinion. For Heidegger, it is our consciousness of our own mortality that acts like a religious vocation: it galvanizes us into realizing that we must make something of our lives while we have time.

12. Fear of Being

Being is a temporal outpouring – piecemeal, bit by bit, just in time – of pure hap. There are no substances, in the sense of beings that are independent of time and chance and are corrosion-proof. On the contrary, everything is contingent, everything is happenstance, everything is Becoming, everything comes to be and then passes away. Not everything is entirely random however, for on the large scale the way of things often happens to drop into habits, including even some self-perpetuating habits. Once these are established they may accumulate, and may take on the appearance of laws; but 'historically' they are just self-perpetuating habits that Nature fell into and got stuck with. In Nature as in Society there is a creeping process by which accidents and improvizations turn into customs, habits, traditions and even mathematical laws. So in the realm of Being it can happen that a combination of large-scale statistical regularities and self-perpetuating habits gives to our life a measure of constancy and predictability which is sweet enough – and for much of the time very sweet indeed. It is by no means true that we are all of us always afraid of time as such, for we seem to have a 'natural' appetite for life and we relish the changing flux of sense-experience. Any unchanged stimulus grows numb or dull after a while, but variation refreshes the senses. Evidently we have a strong biologically-inbuilt enjoyment of the temporal flow of life.

As for the stability of our world, the whole of human cultural life, from the very beginnings of symbolic communication and social custom, has involved the development of an enormous apparatus of customs, conventions, rules, traditions, habits and laws, all of which are designed to regularize and stabilize life as far as possible. Modern Western society has become quite astonishingly minutely and well administered. This development has been made possible by the development of double-entry book-keeping, filing-systems and other devices of the modern state, suddenly and hugely enhanced in the twentieth century by the harnessing of electricity and the arrival of high-speed communications, and now the new information technologies. In 'the West', at least, our lives have become on average very much longer, more comfortable and predictable than ever before. It does not surprise you in the least that your supermarket manager has no problem at all in maintaining stocks of around 10,000 product lines from all over the world, all the year round. Dozens of times a day, a computer somewhere notes us doing something.

When life has become so stable for most people, a number of our ancient biological responses become almost redundant. They include aggression, anxiety, and the circadian rising and lowering of our moods. These leftover responses and moods are evidently very troublesome, because almost everyone makes some use of drugs, whether socially-regulated or medically-prescribed or simply illegal, to help manage them. And it is not surprising that the fears and anxieties which surround life's remaining uncertainties have become all the more intense. We remain vulnerable to the breakdown of our closest relationships, to political or economic upheaval, to crime and accident, to the sudden onset of debilitating or terminal illness, and above all, to death.

We are also deeply troubled – more deeply than we understand – by a sense of loss. Consider this contrast: in India amongst the very poor one may still find many lives that are made bearable and given dignity by religion. In the West, life is made predictable and comfortable by management. The Indian is not troubled by a deep sense of loss; but the Westerner is, and now cannot think of any way in which that fearful loss can ever again be made good. We seem to have suffered a massive and permanent cognitive and emotional loss, and it has left a hole in our hearts. Otherwise, we are doing fine. Just getting organized – getting knowledge organized, and getting problem-solving organized – has given us the vast edifice of modern science and technology, and the formidable efficiency of modern administration. It has transformed the human situation, but at a heavy cost. Human provision for the future is already far more efficient than divine providence ever was, modern Western medicine is much more reliable than sacramental healing or a visit to Lourdes, and agricultural science produces far bigger harvests than fertility rites ever achieved. Just getting ourselves organized has brought about the twilight of the gods. That is all it took.

There is, however, an unhappy side-effect. The more we succeed in engineering the risk and hardship out of life, the more horror and dread we feel in the face of the residue that we haven't yet been able to manage out of existence, and perhaps never will. The risks may have been greatly reduced, but they still exist. Death has been pretty effectively postponed, but it still comes to us all. We have created a society so dominated by technology, and therefore so preoccupied with means, that our vision of the ends of life has become foggy. In the most advanced societies very many people live in quiet despair. Mass unhappiness is without a doubt going to become the next great political issue: but what is to be done about it?

It might be thought that we ought still to be able to look to religion to deal with the residual problems of life that technology cannot manage away. But that will not work: the old kind of religion that flourished between about −500 and +1660 CE now exists only in ironized, bracketed form. It is a much-loved and jealously-preserved relic, but nobody in the world can now believe, or will ever again be able to believe, in the way people believed until about the time of John Bunyan. Metaphysical horror and despair in the face of life's uncertainty and death's certainty is now just as acutely-felt within religious communities as outside them.[1]

The Fear of Being, I am saying, is our postmodern disorder in the face of the triumph of technology and the twilight of the gods. The world has become just a streaming flux of signs, empty of substance, empty of fixed points and stable values.[2] It comes from nowhere and it is going nowhere. We ourselves are only temporary clearing-houses, receiving, storing, sending out our messages. Soon we – or at any rate, I – will be no more. The Fear of Being is horror and despair in the face of the new post-modern vision of the human condition that has gradually emerged and triumphed in the West since the end of the First World War, and the breakdown of all the old spiritual resources by which we might have sought to cope with it. The triumph of technology turns out to be the triumph of nihilism and despair.

We can't go back, either to metaphysics or to fundamental-ism. The culture is now post-philosophical (which makes me wonder about the prospects for this little book). There is no way back, and no source from which we might gain supple-mentary information to the effect that everything is after all better than it seems on the surface. Nowadays there *is* only the surface: first impressions are the only impressions. Everything is just what it seems, because there *is* only seeming.

So what we need is a conversion of ourselves, from the Fear of Being to the Love of Being. Being (B̶e̶i̶n̶g̶, Be(com)ing, Be-ing) is simply life's outpouring of pure transient contingency, coming from nowhere, flickering and passing, going nowhere. We tried to get Being under control, to regulate it. Following hints from the extent to which Nature herself has dropped into routines like that of day and night, we tried to master and regularize our life as completely as possible. We did remarkably well. But the better we did, the more obvious it became that we could never succeed completely, and the more terrified we became of the unmasterable residue.

But is it really unmasterable? Alan Harrington, in an uncomfortable and perhaps now almost forgotten book,[3] argued that by the 1960s the overwhelming triumphs of technology in all other areas were leaving humankind more and more terrified of ageing and death, and less and less able to gain any consolation at all from the traditional sources of it in religion and philosophy. He concluded, like the poet of *Die Winterreise*, that 'we must become gods ourselves', by a programme of scientific research aimed at the conquest of ageing and death. Harrington thought it could be done, and he wrote thirty years ago. Since then great advances in biotechnology have made his proposal sound much more practicable than it did in the late Sixties. So let us suppose that the genes controlling ageing can be isolated and modified. Would earthly immortality and an abundance of high-tech comforts and resources actually cure the religious condition that I am calling the Fear of Being?

No, it would not, and for approximately the Buddha's reasons. For the problem lies not with ageing and death but rather with that in us which is terrified of ageing and death, and which simply cannot reconcile itself to temporality and contingency. The self that wants to be a substance wants to separate Being from Becoming; it wants to get free of time. It is afraid not just of death, but of transience itself and as such. It is horrified by the way everything *passes*, so that nothing is ever completely present and fully possessed. (Weren't many of our old religious dreams in fact merely dreams of absolute and secure *possession* and *control* ?) But the fear of transience itself and as such is not remediable by changing anything outside ourselves. No technical fix can cure it.

13. The Love of Being

One aspect of the July 1997 event has not yet been discussed: in it, the boundary between the self and the world – so far as there is one at all – becomes blurred. Subjectivity is sucked out into objectivity. One disappears out into and then drowns in the Object. One is rapt (i.e., snatched away) or absorbed; and it is this merger of the self with the world that creates such a powerful effect of happiness.

The idioms that we use make matters a little clearer. 'See Naples and die': one feels either that one is dying, or that one suddenly and intensely wishes to die, of happiness. 'My heart goes out': the violent, surging feeling of faintness and dizziness here is especially associated with certain painters and certain landscapes, such as clifftops and hilltops, where we have a long view ahead of us but very little foreground, and our feeling is drawn out into the vast intervening space. We may feel a great desire to plunge down into the void. In traditional religion the voiding of the self into objectivity and nothingness is usually associated with prolonged and very still meditation, perhaps aided by some such figure as an icon, a cross or a mandala. The aim is to slow language and thought down into emptiness. Certainly one can by this means reach a certain voiding of subjectivity, but it takes a very long time, and great patience; whereas what I shall describe as the Love of Being reaches the same result in *seconds*. One simply yields oneself up or opens oneself, in the moment or *at once*, to pure sensuous immediacy; no, more than that, to the purely contingent moment-by-moment forthcoming of Becoming. The aim is to stop thinking, to stop actively putting-a-construction-upon-experience, and to give oneself completely just to the Be-ing of Being. Some works of art, and some landscapes, seem to help us to do this; they appear to glow, or even to *tremble* as if they are alive. I have seen this latter effect most vividly in certain *pointilliste* beach scenes.

We can also profitably call upon the aid of creatures such as insects and the smaller songbirds, that live more in immediacy and at a much higher pace than we do. Consider the intense quivering vitality of the bird or the insect, not as a reminder, but as a *de*minder. If you empathize with it, it will draw you up to its speed and so out of your sluggish reflective self and into Being. As the English idioms again show, 'mind' is associated with anxiety, pain and care, and with being wound up. Do you mind? If so, you will recognize the happiness of becoming unwound or deminded. 'Mind' is *care*, and even a state of paralysed indecision, and we may need to be drawn out of it.

When we are 'sent' or entranced, and find ourselves lost in Being, we drown in outpouring, foundationless secondariness. We disappear into the outpouring flux of everything. The self as substance and as self-conscious individual subject happily vanishes. But objectivity disappears as well; hence the phrase used elsewhere, 'the double meltdown'.[1] In the mystical tradition, the double meltdown is typically presented or represented by means of a play upon the ambiguity of the phrase 'the love of God', *Amor Dei*. This phrase might signify the love of God towards the creature; or the responding love of the creature for God; or it may invoke the neither-subject-nor-object flux of loving into which *both* God *and* the creature are melted down. The ambiguity here between the subjective and the objective genitive links religion and sex in a way that has always been found delightful. As I make you mine, you make me yours, and we both yield to something that is prior to either of us, and engulfs both of us. The triple meaning of the phrase 'the love of

God' (our love for God, God's love for us, and the divinity of Love itself in which everything suffers meltdown) is not only erotically delightful, but also *theologically* delightful, because of the way it allows us to insinuate the erotic subversion of orthodoxy whilst yet retaining 'plausible deniability'. Dante gives it to us in a few brief lines, at the end of the *Paradiso* (XXXIII, 142ff.). He cannot find words to describe the vision in which his great work culminates, except perhaps through the image of a wheel in the rotation of which each thing turns round into its opposite, and the creature's love for God becomes the same thing as God's love for the creature, that which turns everything:

All' alta fantasia qui mancò possa:
    ma già volgeva il mio disiro e il *velle*
    sì come rota ch'egualmente è mossa

l'amor che move il sole e l'altre stelle.[2]

. . . this lofty vision was beyond my powers; but already my desire and will were rolled – as a great wheel turns equally – by the love that moves the sun and the other stars.

In effect, Be-ing is the universal love into which both God and the creature are melted down.

To the soberer sort of analytical philosopher the foregoing paragraphs may seem to have been contentless religious gush, too emotive to be of serious philosophical interest. But when modern Anglo-Saxon philosophy assumes its supercool and professional tone of voice, it cuts itself off from its own history. For just as the great German philosophers remained profoundly influenced by Paul and Luther even as they were secularizing them, so the English-speaking philosophers remained 'mystical' religious naturalists, religiously in love, like all the British and certainly like me, with Nature and the sense of sight even as they were busy transforming the old theological vision of the world into the new 'experimental philosophy' (i.e., science). They might or might not break with orthodoxy, and they might even become explicit atheists, but they almost always remain religious in their feeling for the sense of sight and for Nature, gardened by Man.

Thus Thomas Hobbes – not unlike Lucretius – is an 'energetic' naturalist, with an expressivist view of religious language. George Berkeley is a religious phenomenalist. He sees the world as an outpouring and unceasing stream of phenomena that can be read as a 'divine visual language'. It is a pity that he doesn't provide for the meltdown of his perceivers into the flux of the perceived. Above all, the young David Hume's version of religious naturalism is not very far from what I have been describing.[3] For him as for Berkeley, philosophy begins with simply the flux of phenomena, or 'perceptions'. Every perception seems to be a distinct entity. The senses do not perceive whatever it is that glues the world's constituents together, and neither does reason intuit any objective logical reactions between perceptions. So how can we explain the belief that we all have and would find it very hard to do without, namely, the belief that we have a coherent and orderly physical world about us?

Hume sets aside, as being too obviously implausible, what he calls 'The opinion of a double existence and representation'. By that, he means the theory that there are two orders of existence, the mental and the physical. On this view, the mind is made to be a mirror of the outside world. Things and events in the physical world generate perceptions in our organs of sense which are conveyed into the mind and there assembled into a representation, or mental model, of the external world.

So what Hume is talking about when he refers to 'a double existence and representation' is the theory associated with Descartes and Locke: the theory that perception enables us to build up in the mental world a model or representation of the way things are out there in the physical world. Hume thinks that this theory is overcomplicated.[4] Ordinary people – 'the vulgar' – see 'only one being', and believe what they see. Hume proposes to begin, at least, by going along with the vulgar. There is only one being. So he starts with 'perceptions', and asks how we can get from them to the picture of the orderly and coherent world about us. And his answer of course is that if the world is not held together either by anything sensible, or by anything purely rational, the only remaining possibility is that we ourselves *impute* all the cement. Our imagination, our customs and expectations, and our feelings supply *all* the glue that sticks the world together. On the basis of custom, we impute to clusters of perceptions their unity, and to successive perceptions their causal connections. In short, the world we see is a world we built, and apart from that there's nothing to be said except that we have no feasible option but to note that it works out well enough in practice, and to accept our own natural belief in its 'reality'.

The position that Hume reaches is subtle, and has some interesting affinities. Like Berkeley, he is not above appealing to the opinion of what he calls 'the vulgar' or 'the generality of mankind', and Berkeley calls 'commonsense'. He is proto-Kantian, in that he sees the world before our eyes as the product of two principles: *perceptions* and *custom*, foreshadowing Kant's *intuitions* and *concepts*. And, as David Pears notes, he looks forward to Wittgenstein's 'subtle positivism' (or 'quietism') in being ready to admit that in the end we cannot do better or know more than what's already open to everyone in ordinary language and everyday life. And I would make the same point: philosophers and religious writers must give up any pretensions to be some kind of gnostic or seer who has found the way to a Higher Truth. All such claims are bogus. Ordinariness is abyssal. Nothing in all philosophy can surpass the subtlety and beauty of the most ordinary English idioms: take a while, for example, to meditate upon the phrases give *in*, give *up*, give *out*, give *away*. In each case, attend to what the preposition does. These everyday phrases open the most amazing religious depths. Now try the exercise of finding similar beauties in the standard idioms that use the verbs *pass*, *make* and *burn*. Write them down. Pass by, pass on, pass out, pass over, pass away. Burn up, burn out. However long the human race survives, nobody will ever do better than that. How *could* one? Since we are made in and by the motion of language running in and through us, we cannot hope to do better than it does. Language itself says it all. So on my account, thinking is waiting upon Language, as prayer is waiting upon Being.

In the British philosophical tradition at its best, the Love of Being appears as a return *after* scepticism, *after* reflection, *after* metaphysics, back into ordinariness; ordinariness now perceived as being religiously very deep, and as the product of a combination of principles. Before Hume, it had for a very long time been customary to look for a single *arché* behind the world: a single sovereign controlling principle that was at once the world's Beginning, the world-Ground and the final Explanation of everything; usually, but not quite always, God. But now Hume, an historically-minded Tory sceptic, begins to open up the idea that our world-view itself is a mixed product, made of perceptions and custom, combining what is given to the senses with our own historically-evolved consensus way of interpreting it. The world of Man is thus humankind's prime cultural product. We are the *demiourgoi*,[5] the craftspeople, of our world.

What makes this realization such a happy one? The closest analogy is to be found in those landscape paintings and those gardens that seem to offer a promise of redemption and blessedness by the way they harmonize man and nature. A fruitful, domesticated world is easy on the eye, a happy valley. Hume, rather similarly, moves away from the old view of the world as a theatre or display of divine glory, wisdom and (perhaps) goodness, towards a new view of the world as being something more like a city – something a large number of human beings have collectively evolved over a long period.

In Hume's view, then, our human world is a synthesis of 'perceptions' and 'customs', of something that is sheerly-given together with our own tried, tested and accumulated habits and customary ways of interpreting it. While still in his twenties, he is happy because he is liberated from the extreme theological terrorism in which he was raised. We need not feel in any way guilty and alienated; on the contrary, we are fully entitled to feel completely at ease, and at home in our own world.

I am suggesting, then, that religion and the religious object were already beginning to change even as far back as Hume, in the early 1730s. In the old religion, which reached its culminating form in Islam and in Calvinism, *everything* was traced back to the omnipotent Will of a single Monarch. Faith involved submission and an unconditional commitment of the human will to be henceforth the instrument of the divine Will, the sword of the Lord. In the new religion, the world is an evolving co-operative product and the relation to the religious object does not involve submission so much as patient responsiveness and partnership. As I've suggested elsewhere, Being is still an abyssal mystery, prior to language and never fully grasped. But it gives itself to us, and becomes history in and through us. 'Man is Being's poem', says Heidegger, meaning that as Sein comes out into expression in *Dasein* – concrete, situated human being – it becomes *incarnate*.

14. The Secular Trinity

In the Religion of Being everything is brought down into time, into transience. Everything is 'phenomenalized', by which I mean that it is put up on the screen, and seen as part of the passing show of all existence. The resulting world view is often called nihilistic, but it is where we are now, and it is not irreligious. Far from it: indeed, I have been hinting that the Revelation of Being is a naturalized and temporalized version of what in earlier times was described as the Vision of God. Although I have phrased the discussion in terms of an event in my own life and dated it in July 1997, this was purely a matter of convenience, and one might equally well have phrased it all in terms of a late Van Gogh painting – there being no doubt that Vincent's art represents a powerful secularization or temporalization of an originally Christian vision. Towards the end, he was painting the Revelation of Being and solar living every day.

I have also suggested that Martin Heidegger's rather 'mystical' late philosophy of Being, Man and Language represents a very striking transformation of the classical Christian dogma of the Trinity.[1] In Christian thought God the Father is the abyssal fountain of deity (*fons deitatis*); the Son is his 'poem', his perfect self-expression, begotten in his heart from all eternity and now incarnate in Man, for Man, for evermore; and the Spirit, the Lord and giver of life that forms and animates everything, is Language itself, pictured of course as winged – as a dove – and as representing the *vinculum amoris*, the bond of love that both springs from and unites the Father and the Son.[2] More interestingly than any previous attempt at demythologizing religious belief, the *schema* Being, Man and Language presents the whole of 'reality' as a secularization of the Triune God.

Bringing God down into time as Be-ing has had the side-effect of somewhat feminizing God. One reason for this is that standard Christian doctrine was highly patriarchal and pre-scientific. In ancient thought and in Aristotelian biology all creativity was ascribed to the masculine principle alone. Man was to Woman as sower to soil. *Sperma* is the Greek word for seed, and *semen* the Latin, and until the discovery of the mammalian ovum, and then the rise of modern genetics in the late-nineteenth century, the assumption was that Woman made no creative contribution. Her body was like a gardener's indoor propagator, in which she germinated Man's seed, and then after expelling it into the outside world it was she who continued to nurse and tend it.

All these agricultural metaphors remain extraordinarily persistent. Think of the relatively modern English word 'nursery-man'. One might say that in traditional thought Woman was created to be Man's nurseryman. She germinated and raised his seed: in her own person she was both garden and gardener. Hence the image of Mary as a walled garden, a *hortus conclusus*, in mediaeval art. At any rate, traditional philosophical theism pictured God as masculine, and Nature or the earth as feminine. The relation of Man to Woman was even a stock symbol of transcendence (and not only in John Milton's thought). Against this background, if God is finitized or secularized, God will be brought much closer to Nature or to life, and therefore will be symbolically feminized. 'Creation out of nothing', *creatio ex nihilo*, may then come to be seen in terms of 'birthing', or giving birth.

Another effect of the changes that have been taking place in religious thought recently is *laicization*. I take from a well-known reference book's first eight chapter titles a list of what are commonly described as 'the (great) world religions': Judaism, Christianity, Islam, Zoroastrianism, Hinduism, Sikhism, Jainism, Buddhism. At least 90% of what comes up for discussion under these eight chapter-headings is in each tradition the accumulated legacy of the life and work of an élite corps of male religious professionals. The Founder may have been a lay person, but he was scarcely cold in his grave (or perhaps rather, scarcely out of this world) before the professionals had seized power. Since then, they've done almost everything. They have ruled the community, controlling faith and worship, fighting all the battles amongst themselves, and writing almost all the books. They have been a mixed group of people, bishops, monks, professors and others; but it is they who over the centuries have developed the complex, objectified and highly-ideological constructs that are now described as 'Christianity', or 'Buddhism'.

The language still reflects this state of affairs. In popular English idiom, 'the Church' is the clergy as a corporation, and 'going into the Church' is being ordained. Lay persons figure only as members of 'flocks' (in Latin, *congregationes*, from *gregis*, a flock). Church history is history of the clergy, and, with them, of the few other 'ecclesiastical persons'. Theology is and always has been the clerical ideology by means of which the professionals justify and seek to extend their power. Theologians are perceived on all sides as persons employed to work as spin-doctors in the service of the clerical power-structure.

So it always has been, and so to some extent it still is. The 'decline of religion' doesn't exactly mean that people in general have become less religious (they haven't), but rather that nearly everywhere the great corporations of religious professionals are much less powerful than they used to be. Secularization expropriates the clergy, and (religiously-speaking) emancipates and empowers the profane or lay person.

I need not labour all this. I mention it only to raise the

question: 'Can we in retrospect identify an authentic lay tradition in each of the major culture-areas?'

That raises the further question: 'By what criteria might we expect to be able to pick it out?' Since the clerical tradition is preoccupied with power, predominantly male, and makes a clear contrast between its own exalted sphere (the Sacred) and that of the laity (the Secular or profane), then one might expect the lay tradition to make moral criticisms of the power and wealth of the clergy, and to seek by mystical means to evade their priestly claims to monopoly control of everything necessary to salvation. The laity will praise lay life, and indeed domestic life. They will defend woman, the passions, children, poetry, and naturalism in art.

By using such criteria, one may be able to trace a continuous – but at some points rather thin – tradition of genuinely lay religious expression throughout the Latin Christian Middle Ages. For example, I have suggested elsewhere that much of what is nowadays called the 'mystical' tradition represents a tradition of thinly-veiled lay religious protest against the higher clergy's claim to have divine authority to set up roadblocks and collect fees all along the Way to salvation.[3] One may also reasonably claim that something of this-worldly and lay values was successfully preserved in the tradition of secular poetry. Helen Waddell wrote two famous books, *Mediaeval Latin Lyrics* and *The Wandering Scholars*, about these writers.[4] But I am now inclined rather to suggest that it is in the long tradition of mediaeval sculpture – running in Britain from c.650–1540 – that we see the most accessible and convincing evidence of the layman's point of view. The sculptor's was not a distinct and honoured craft and, until terms like *imageur* and *imaginator* came into use in the thirteenth century, there was no word for the trade. No stone carver of the Middle Ages is known to have been a cleric and the only well-known critical discussion of mediaeval sculpture by a contemporary clerical intellectual is the vitriolic condemnation of it by Bernard, Abbot of Clairvaux, whose influence was so powerful that the great Cistercian abbey churches are devoid of any sculptural decoration.[5]

Elsewhere, only a small fraction of the work of the stone carvers now survives, and what remains is very often damaged. Its colouring has gone. But sculpture is unlike stained glass or even painting in that it does not readily lend itself to a Platonic interpretation. One cannot easily claim that it is a 'transparent' icon through which – as in George Herbert's poem – one may 'espy' a heavenly verity. Even when it treats an expressly-religious subject, all sculpture remains obstinately physical, emotionally provocative and this-worldly.

The sculptural tradition in Britain over the nine centuries of the 'Middle Ages' is often quaint and provincial, and never quite reaches the level of Rheims; but it does frequently reach 'European' quality, and is nearly always intensely attractive to us now. It is secular and humanistic religion, with gawky elongated figures and swaying parallel lines creating a strong emotional charge; and it is the work of illiterate craftsmen, their traceable contribution, still surviving in the fabric of a thousand churches despite clerical indifference and (sometimes) sharp hostility. It says something for the Middle Ages that into so many great churches the carvers were able to slip in a treatment of the favourite topic of the fox preaching to a flock of geese.

How far can comparable lay traditions be picked out elsewhere? The single most striking example is East Asian Buddhism, where something of the metaphysics and the religious temper of the *sangha* (the monastic order), was successfully carried across into many areas of secular life and culture, such as landscape painting, calligraphy, gardening, the tea ceremony, flower arranging, the painting of animals and plants, and even archery.

With these two examples, from Christianity and Buddhism, I introduce a general proposition: in its laicized and secularized forms a great religious tradition may be much more interesting and accessible to us now than it can be in its more usual form as an objectified ideology of the spiritual power of priests and monks. We should not be nostalgic for the mystique of supernatural power and authority once wielded by a pyramid of old men in big hats. There's already been far too much of such nostalgia, just as there have been too many people who have continued to feel emotionally that monarchy is a deeper and better system of government than democracy. I seriously suggest that the process of democratization, laicization, secularization should be seen as religious *emancipation*, not decline. And I truly believe that the Love of transient, contingent Being which has come upon me in my later years is a religious advance upon the Love of God which so filled me from 1952 until 1978 or thereabouts. It is solider and more convincing. And don't let the big hats persuade you otherwise. They care only about what *they* call 'the Church', and we can tell is just their power. When we refocus religion around Being we leave behind us forever our former infatuation with the idea that what humans need more than anything else is to get themselves locked on to a single great concentration of pure spiritual power, at which they will gaze forever.

The Revelation of Being is an immanentization – a bringing down into finitude and time – of the Trinity. Be-ing is the quite-unfathomable continual silent outpouring of everything. It is ineffable, prior to language. It reveals itself in 'Man' – which is what Heidegger calls *Dasein*, namely the lit-up, language-differentiated common human world in which we live, move and have our being. (Notice that I put Man, the concrete universal human, *before* the individual human being such as you or me.) And the circle is completed by Language, the living web of symbolic expression and communication that is the medium of our social and historical life. So Being, Man and Language are the Father, the Son and the Holy Ghost, apprehended in the structure of the way we see what we see before our eyes, now.

Words

I hardly know how to describe the kind of writing I now do. It seems to fall outside standard genres. Is it perhaps *edifying philosophy*, or *religious philosophy*, or *the philosophy of religion*? Is it *theology*, or should I just call it *religious writing*? I like the latter, because I try to operate in a region that is prior to any sort of professionalization, whether academic or religious. I want to escape the 'political' concern for the power-interests of any particular sect or academic 'discipline'. I'd like to be purely inventive and 'democratic'. We live at a time when old institutions, old disciplines and old vocabularies are collapsing. Experimentation and a fresh start are what we need.

In which case, I should surely write without using or echoing any of the historic vocabularies of Western philosophy and theology? Do I not expressly say that I want to escape from metaphysics and supernatural belief, and concentrate my whole attention upon this world and the fleeting moment?

However, things aren't quite as simple as that. I have found that in order to produce a religious effect in writing, I cannot simply *quote* ordinariness. I have to make a detour, rather as an artist or a film-maker does, selecting, playing tricks with lighting, shifting the camera around, distorting or exaggerating ordinariness in this way or that – and then hope that we'll return into ordinariness with our vision refreshed. In short, religious writing seeks to get a 'Martian' view of ordinariness, in order to see it as extraordinary, and then returns into it in such a way as to *brighten* it.

The Revelation of Being

In the case of philosophical and religious writing, this detour is the detour through metaphysics. And that is surely why, when I began to look over my text and pick out words that might need to be explained in a glossary, I repeatedly found echoes of Platonism. Even though we write generations after the death of Plato and the end of metaphysics, we are still in thrall to him. Indeed, the very idea of a glossary is itself highly Platonic. It conjures up the picture of philosophy as a search for the exact definitions of general abstract terms, and of the philosopher as a keen-eyed person with a special talent for descrying 'real' and objective Meanings.

Perhaps the detour must have the effect of conjuring up Plato again; but it is a very queer reverse-love-affair that I should have spent so many years battling to get Plato's system out of mine. His terms are boomerangs; we just can't throw them away. Hence one new technical term, *not* included in the list below: *bloody Plato* (p.18).

absolute   non-relative, independent, self-subsistent, unrestricted, free. From 'absolved', released or liberated.

abyssal   bottomless, ungrounded, foundationless. The metaphor of the cosmos, and of a human knowledge-system, as being like a *building* that needs to be erected upon solid ground or secure foundations was very prominent in Western philosophy until the nineteenth century. Even today many people's instinct is to look for a ground, with the result that we find the realization that the passing show of existence is quite groundless to be, precisely, *abyssal*. The metaphor of an abyss expresses our sense of vertigo. But this dizziness is only dizziness *relative* to our disappointed Western expectation that there really ought to be a ground of everything. If we were good Buddhists we'd not feel dizzy: we'd be happy about everything's Emptiness.

active non-realism my late-1980s philosophy of religion, a postmodernist version of the older existentialist appeal to decision and commitment. After metaphysics, we see a religious faith as a programme for action. If you really want to, you can make it all come true by the way you choose it and live it out.

anthropomonism I first used this term in 1985, as variant upon the use of 'christomonism' to describe Karl Barth's theology. I expand the notion of 'Man', the human realm, to incorporate the whole known and language-traversed world; and then I empty out the human self – and suddenly feel very happy. If you've followed that point, you have understood this book; and even better, you should have grasped it in conjunction with the similar trick I play with the term Language.

arché beginning, first principle, origin, starting-point. 'The myth of the normative origin' is the way of thinking that seeks renewal by returning to the way things were 'in the beginning'. The first state of a thing is thought to be specially pure and authoritative. Compare **telos**, below.

autonomy the condition of being a law unto oneself, or immanently self-ordering.

be(com)ing Platonism makes a contrast between two realms or orders of being: there is timeless self-subsistent Being, and there is the temporal flux of becoming. The former alone is truly Real; the latter is corruptible and unreal. We ought to flee from the realm of becoming and seek our true home in the world of Eternal Being: 'Change and decay in all around I see; / O Thou who changest not, abide with me.'

I conflate the two together to make the portmanteau word be(com)ing. Getting rid of Plato means getting free of the split between Being and becoming. But I've had to expound Plato in order to kick him out; so he has boomeranged back again, as he always does.

Being or ~~Being~~. See *The Religion of Being* (1998). Perhaps best explained as the difference between the completest-possible description of some thing, and that thing's actual existence; provided that you also grasp that this explanation of Being makes it something outside language and therefore a non-word, ~~Being~~.

clear, *clarus* bright, shining, with many lovely cognates. Declare, clear *up*; do I make *myself* clear?

contingent compare the related terms *contiguous, tangential*. Not necessitated, just happening to come about, accidental (= falling out, coming by chance).

Demiurge, demiourgos in Greek, a public worker, from *demios* and *ergon*, an artisan or craftsman. In Plato and in some popular Anglo-Saxon theism to this day, the Demiurge is a finite designer-God who is the world-architect. (In my jargon, this is Designer Realism).

dogma, dogmatic, dogmatism a dogma is a tenet accepted as certainly true and foundational, perhaps because it is considered to be self-evident, or because it is certified by some authority, or (and most commonly nowadays) because dogmatism is thought to be the only alternative to the abyss of scepticism.

ecstasy the state of being outside or beside oneself.

edifying philosophy much nineteenth-century Idealist philosophy, from Hegel to Bradley, was constructed, whether consciously or not, as a substitute for theology. Russell and Moore set out to be resolutely logical and analytical, and to banish such 'edifying philosophy'. They aimed to make philosophy academic and boring. On the European mainland, however, philosophy has mostly continued to be edifying, and so has remained of great interest to the general reader. Since about 1980, edification has been creeping back into English-language philosophy.

entostasy a frivolous coinage of my own, a reverse ecstasy in which we achieve religious joy, not by jumping out of ourselves, but by jumping back into ourselves. The way to blessedness is, not to try to escape from one's own transience and mortality, but to return into it completely, affirming it without regret.

eternity, eternal distinguish two senses. In Platonism, eternity is timelessness, and belongs only to God, the things of God and the eternal world. Every necessary truth is an 'eternal' truth. In Existentialism, 'eternal' is said to be a quality, not an extension. In Romanticism and more recently, eternity is associated with the sublime, the sun and everything that is *solar*. Eternal happiness is 'solar' happiness, a happiness that never wholly forsakes one, however bad things get to be. For the modern/postmodern sense of eternity see, for example, the image of the sun and 'the great noontide' in Turner, Nietzsche, D.H. Lawrence and Bataille.

existence literally standing-forth, but in my text usually 'forthcoming' or 'outpouring', because I want to temporalize existence and see Be-ing as a present participle. In Russell's analysis, existence is simply the having-application of a concept. Following Hume, he avoids any head-on discussion of the question of Being.

final vocabulary the vocabulary in which we explain and justify the beliefs and the values that are of the greatest importance to us. The expression comes from Richard Rorty.

The Revelation of Being

form, formless, formative   Platonism again: the form/matter distinction, says Derrida, 'opens philosophy'. In me it recurs in the relation of Being to Language. Language forms Being as the divine Word once formed Chaos. In fact I can't pretend to escape the form/matter distinction. Plato wins again.

heteronomy   the condition of being subject to a law that transcends oneself; being 'under' the Law.

historicism   a term that incorporates two ideas, one of which we should adopt, and the other we should repudiate: (a) all actual being is intra-historical; and (b) there are ascertainable laws of historical development. (a) is true; (b) is a mess.

immanence   'remaining within', and not looking to or depending upon any external or 'transcendent' authority, foundation or endorsement. Immanence is closely related to 'naturalism', and to my own favorite term 'outsidelessness'. Since about the time of Hegel – i.e., since the early nineteenth century – we have more and more sought to explain things purely immanently. The two most familiar examples of the changeover are history and language.
   Thoroughgoing immanentism is scarcely distinguishable from relativism.

intelligible, noumenal   equivalent terms, because they are the Latin and Greek opposites of *sensible* and *phenomenal*, respectively. Intelligible or noumenal things are objects of the understanding, Forms or Ideas. They were seen by Plato as occupying a really-existent noumenal world. See **noumenal** below.

intuition   direct beholding. The word is used in philosophy in two very different ways. In Kant, intuition is raw, formless sensation. Almost everyone else follows Plato and uses intuition to mean pure, immediate rational 'vision' of necessary Truth, just seeing that what is eternally so is so and must be so.

isomorphous   of the same shape, corresponding or matching point-by-point. The Calvinist/Anglo-Saxon idea of 'literal truth' seems to suppose that a sentence can copy the shape of an extra-linguistic state of affairs.

Language   used here of semiosis, the continuous process of symbolic exchange which is the medium of all human life.

light   in English, extraordinarily resonant, because it inter-weaves two different groups of words and clusters of meta-phors. The *lux, lumen, illuminatio* group of words and meta-phors ramifies around the universal association between optical seeing and intellectual 'seeing' or understanding. I *see*. But there is also the *levis* (opposite of *gravis*) group of words, linking *light* as small, of little weight, of little consequence, airy, high-spirited, and humorous.

logos   Word, thought, discourse, rationale, with very rich theological overtones. In late-ancient-Jewish thought, close to Spirit.

Man   Once more let me explain why and how I extend the notion of 'Man' to incorporate the whole complex world that we have built around ourselves. We define ourselves by developing our language, evolving a continuously-humming network of symbolic exchange through which we each of us become conscious of ourselves as stations on the net, who are both receivers and senders, patients and agents. In our dialogue we differentiate our world of interacting persons and things, spread out in time and space. Describing our world, we *own* or appropriate it, and so define ourselves indirectly *via* our place in our world, our roles and tasks. In short, we should give up the picture of ourselves as having been first made and then inserted into a ready-made world prepared for us; and instead we should see our self-definition and our world-definition as having evolved together, each requiring and presupposing the other. So each person coincides with her own life in her own world, and this *complete* embeddedness of the self in its world, when fully understood and accepted, is supposed by me to create an effect of religious happiness, the love of Being.

mentalese the supposed universal language of thought; believed in, for example, by Aristotle, Leibniz and some moderns – but not by me. Translators do not work *via* any 'mentalese'. And notice the way dreams, poems, jokes and even philosophies are always rooted in particular natural vocabularies.

metaphysics (= 'Platonism') the ancient way of thinking, best expressed by Plato, which divides eternal Being from temporal becoming. Every complex domain or class in the realm of becoming is unified in, grounded in, and governed by its eternal archetype (or Idea) in the realm of eternal Being.

naturalism, religious naturalism especially, the attempt to understand the realm of becoming as 'Nature' and to explain it and everything in it 'immanently', or 'naturalistically' – that is, without having recourse to another and superior realm outside it. Darwin's theory of the *Origin of Species* is perhaps the most interesting and powerful of all naturalistic theories.

necessity what is necessary cannot be otherwise. Moral necessitation is overriding moral constraint to do such and such: physical necessitation is physical constraint by antecedent causal conditions.

nihilism a vague term. In the nineteenth century, it originally meant little more than the denial of standard views in religion and morals. Philosophically, usually denial of all substance, both finite and infinite. Nietzsche's chief emphasis is upon the denial of values.

noumenal equivalent to 'intelligible', with a contrast between the 'apparent' sensible world below and the 'real' intelligible world above, in which Plato locates all noumenal things. For Kant, things considered in themselves, and apart from our knowledge of them, are noumenal and, as such, unknowable.

objective thrown out there, over against us. **Objectivism** is in effect equivalent to realism.

phenomena shinings, seemings, appearances; fleeting scraps of sense-experience, called by Hume 'impressions'.

possible capable of happening or being done or existing. The realm of the possible is the whole realm of what may or may not be so; the contingent realm is the (smaller) domain of what, as it has turned out, happens to be so.

postmodernism in the late Middle Ages the *devotio moderna* was religious devotion to the human Jesus. Modernity from Descartes to Marx was typically man-centred: it sought to view all reality, and to justify knowledge, from the point of view of the human subject. It tended to view all history as a 'grand narrative' of progressive human liberation by the growth of Enlightenment, or by political change, or (since about 1893) by technological advances. Modernity was typically optimistic about the long-term human prospect, and realistic in world-view and ethics.

Postmodernity is the cultural epoch that begins as all these ideas break down. It is most clearly foreshadowed by the work of Nietzsche in the 1880s and by Dada and Surrealism after

World War One. Postmodernity finds no logic in history; it is very often anti-realistic to the point of nihilism; it tends to reduce everything to a play of signs on a flat surface such as a screen, or our skin; and it is self-consciously paradoxical.

qualia   'feels' or scraps of experience that have such-and-such a quality.

realism   typically, and Platonically, belief in objective and publicly authoritative norms of truth, meaning and value. By extension, the belief that there is a fully-formed and intelligible order of things, a real world, out there and independent of our consciousness (or our language). From Descartes onwards much of modern philosophy was preoccupied with vindicating realism, in the sense of the objectivity of human knowledge, against sceptical attack.

The story of the breakdown of realism goes back as far as Kant and the German Idealist philosophers, but nowadays tends to focus upon the work of Nietzsche, whose vast importance has been recognised since 1956 even by Anglo-Saxons. Post-realistic philosophy has tended to move towards either pragmatism or 'semiotic materialism', the philosophy of language or of the sign. Post-realistic religious thought has tended to move towards either non-dogmatic religious pragmatism or Buddhism. But perhaps Realism, like Plato, will always tend to come back, because you can't explain any other philosophy without explaining it – and therefore reviving it.

redemption   liberation from bondage, or pawn, or evil.

secondariness   consequential, or dependent, or 'secondary' existence, like that of the Cheshire Cat's grin.

self-subsistence   the state of being radically independent and oneself the only and sufficient cause of one's own existence: also, *aseity*, 'from-oneself-ness'.

sense-datum, sense-impression   The atom of sense-experience, considered as something sheerly-given, a *datum*; or as something impressed upon our sensibility or sensory surface, as a seal makes an impression upon wax.

sign   any conventional symbol by means of which some kind of message or instruction is conveyed. In our own media-led, advertising and fashion-led culture all consumer goods have become charged with symbolic meanings, and a company logo may be a very valuable saleable commodity.

spirituality   a vague and contested word now. Perhaps, the collection of regular practices and forms of expression through which we may seek to get ourselves together, represent our feeling for the human condition, and find personal happiness.

subjective   thrown under or within; pertaining to the point of view and the 'private' feelings of the individual human person.

substance   standing under or within; Greek, 'hypostasis'. Unified independent being. The metaphysical principle that 'stands under' and 'holds together' an individual thing's collection of qualities and attributes.

system   any organized and interconnected body of knowledge or group of objects.

telos   Greek for goal or end, the word conjoining the ideas of last-in-time and perfection or fulfilment. The word itself encourages the old belief that history itself is like a great story, with a beginning and an End or Goal.

temporality   time-bound-ness.

transient   literally: going-by, passing.

void   an ambiguous term, used sometimes to mean empty space and metaphorical emptiness generally, and sometimes to mean 'emptiness – even of space, too', i.e. absolute emptiness and nothingness. In which case, 'voidism' might turn out to be a doctrine that simply asks us to give up all speculative thinking, because there is nothing for such thinking to discover.

Notes

Foreword

1. For an explanation of the term 'final vocabulary', see Richard Rorty, *Contingency, Irony, and Solidarity*, Cambridge: Cambridge University Press 1989, c.4, pp.73ff.

2. It may be claimed that G.E. Lessing (1729–1781) was a pluralist (of sorts) before Kierkegaard. See *Nathan the Wise* (1779), etc.

3. For perception as making out, see pp.21f.

4. Andrew Bowie, *From Romanticism to Critical Theory: The Philosophy of German Literary Theory*, London: Routledge 1997, discusses the idea that literature and art work by 'defamiliarization and return', and sees it as still being influential in Heidegger's idea of the 'world-disclosing' power of the work of art.

2. Being

1. Philosophical and scientific theories often run interestingly parallel, and there is an especially striking analogy between our doctrine of Being as an efflux of pure contingency, and the well-known doctrine in modern physics that even in a vacuum at absolute zero there are 'quantum fluctuations' of matter/energy.

This doctrine follows from Heisenberg's uncertainty principle (1927). Even at absolute zero, a particle must still be jittering about; for if it were at a complete standstill, its momentum and position would both be determinable precisely and simultaneously – which would violate the uncertainty principle. But energy and time also obey Heisenberg's rule, so that there must be quantum fluctuations of energy even in the vacuum. And such fluctuation must be able to create particles. These particles must be produced briefly, in the form of short-lived matter/antimatter twins.

A consequence of the theory is the so-called 'Casimir effect', the tendency of a pair of very flat parallel metal plates to stick together, even in a vacuum at very low temperature. This phenomenon has been demonstrated experimentally.

The philosophically-interesting corollary of all this is that it seems to violate an old maxim in theistic metaphysics: *ex nihilo nihil fit*, nothing can come into being out of nothing. This maxim has always been prominent in theistic apologetics. It has been argued that our purely-contingent world cannot have come into being all by itself; it must have been created, or it needs to be explained as the product of a non-contingent World-Ground. But it now seems that all arguments of this type are obsolete. We can do without the twin ideas of absolute or necessary Being and absolute Nothingness, and instead see everything as having arisen by chance, in time, out of minute fluctuations in the void. In philosophical terms, we dispense both with absolute Being and with absolute Nothingness, and say instead that there is everywhere and always just the outpouring of Be-ing, pure hap, or Be(com)ing. *In re* there are no hard and fast lines, and no absolutes. Instead, there is everywhere wobbling, fluctuation, and a dance of probabilities.

For the scientific principles involved here, see Philip Yam's article in *Scientific American*, December 1997, pp.54ff., upon which I have drawn.

2. Pessimism in its modern form derives from Schopenhauer, *ennui* from Flaubert, nihilism from Nietzsche and *anomie* from Durkheim. Anxiety (German, *Angst*; Danish, *Angest*) was put on the map above all by Kierkegaard, *The Concept of Anxiety*, 1844.

3. Man

1. Karl Marx, 'Towards a Critique of Hegel's *Philosophy of Right*: Introduction'; quoted from David McLellan (ed.), *Karl Marx: Selected Writings*, Oxford: Oxford University Press 1977, p.63.

2. David Hume, *A Treatise of Human Nature*, ed. L.A. Selby-Bigge, Oxford: Clarendon Press 1888 and many later editions, p.252: see also pp.633ff.; and in the Analytical Index, p.667, s.v. 'Identity'.

3. Ibid., p.253.

4. Ibid., p.259.

5. In the late Victorian novel, the best example of this is perhaps Henry James; in the early Victorian period, *Wuthering Heights* (1847) stands out. Emily Brontë the author is entirely effaced, and the main storyteller is Lockwood; but he in turn employs a sub-narrator, the housekeeper Nelly Dean.

The very varied devices that novelists have used in order to hide themselves and make their stories seem the more veracious offer an extraordinary and fascinating fund of analogies for the relation between the human self and its world. How can philosophers have missed something so big and interesting?

6. Consider here also those many paintings by Magritte in which the painter himself appears as only the back of his own very conventional head. Magritte very wittily indeed observes that when this figure looks into the mirror, he *still* sees only the back of his own head. That is correct.

7. See Charles Taylor, *Sources of the Self: The Making of the Modern Identity*, Cambridge: Cambridge University Press 1989; Robert C. Solomon, *Continental Philosophy since 1750: The Rise and Fall of the Self*, A History of Western Philosophy, Volume 7, Oxford: Oxford University Press 1988; and also the last writings of Walter Kaufmann, especially his three volume *Discovering the Mind*, London: McGraw-Hill 1980.

4. Language

1. See Josef Simon, *Philosophy of the Sign* (German first edition, Berlin: Walter de Gruyter 1989; Eng. trans. George Heffernan, New York: SUNY 1995), for a good example of a thoroughgoing philosophy of the sign.

In this connection, it is worth remarking that in *philosophy* at least, 'postmodernism' is the view that treats all reality as a process of signs. Exponents of such a view include, for example, Eco in Italy, Simon in Germany, and Baudrillard in France. See in particular, Umberto Eco, *Semiotics and the Philosophy of Language*, London: Macmillan 1984.

2. Cited from C.H. Dodd, *The Interpretation of the Fourth Gospel*, Cambridge: Cambridge University Press 1954, p.275.

3. Wilhelm von Humboldt, *On the Diversity of the Structure of Human Language and its Influence on the Intellectual Development of*

Mankind (1836), section 8: 'Language . . . is perpetually and at every moment something *transitory* . . . Language itself is not a work (*ergon*), but an activity (*energeia*).' This passage is quoted and discussed by Heidegger in his late essay *On the Way to Language* (1959; Eng. trans. Peter D. Hertz and Joan Stambaugh, New York: Harper and Row 1971).

5. Being and Man

1. Josef Simon, *The Philosophy of the Sign* (cited above, c.4, n.1), especially sections 1 and 11.

2. Simon admits this difficulty: 'A philosophy of the sign is possible today . . . only in the language of metaphysics' (p.32). As a result, postmodern philosophy can't help looking like idealism: 'Idealism is to this extent the truth of metaphysics' (p.35). But Simon sticks to his philosophy of the sign-alone, whereas I prefer the triad Being, Man and Language, for the reasons given here and in c.7, below.

3. *Revelation* 21.15–21.

6. Being and Language

1. From 'On the Way to Language', in David Farrell Krell (ed.), *Martin Heidegger: Basic Writings*, revised and expanded edition, London: Routledge 1994, p.424.

2. J.L. Austin, *How to Do Things with Words*, Oxford: Oxford University Press 1975. In his day Austin was perceived as making rather an original point about language, and a good deal of 'speech-act theory' developed out of his work. In fact, Austin was reviving ideas about the executive force of language that were very prominent in pre-scientific culture – for example, in the Hebrew Bible's ideas about the Word of God and the words of prophets, and in Christian liturgy and sacramental theology. Why were these things overlooked for so long? There were two main reasons: first, from Descartes to Wittgenstein the dominance of science led people to regard the disengaged observer's view of the world as the best view of it, and his disciplined purely-descriptive use of language as the best sort of speech; and secondly, at Oxford and elsewhere during the same period the study of languages was dominated by the study of *dead* languages. Under these conditions people easily lost the sense of language-use as world-building *activity*.

7. Man and Language

1. *Language as a power*: some friends object to my description of Language as auto-mobile, self-moving and always in motion. They think it sounds animistic. They say that language doesn't move until a person moves it. This text, for example, is not moving while the book is sitting shut up on the shelf: it moves when, and only when, the book is taken down, opened and read.

Eco starts from this very point. He distinguishes the *sign*, seen as being 'stiff' and paired or correlated with its own meaning, from *semiosis*, seen as a process or activity; and then he brings the two ideas together, so that 'the semiosic process of interpretation is present at the very core of the concept of the sign'. 'There is therefore no opposition between the "nomadism" of semiosis (and of interpretative activity) and the alleged stiffness and immobility of the sign' (Eco, *Semiotics* [c.4, n.1 above], p.1).

That is correct. Language explains itself *ambulando*, as it trundles along. The meaning of a word that is new to us is supplied by the rest of the run of language of which it is part. It is in this way that hundreds of new words are introduced into the English language every year, and *become current*. They *catch on*, insofar as it is obvious that they are doing a definite and useful job, *before* there is any authoritative definition of them that can be consulted. At this early stage, they have to make themselves plain *ambulando*; and it is only *after* a word has *established its currency* without a dictionary that a lexicographer comes along, observes its currency and writes a dictionary entry describing it. Meaning is always *first* currency, and only *then* a definition.

These simple considerations are enough to demythologize for ever the old realist or 'Platonic' notion of what a meaning is; and they open the way to the thoroughgoing postmodernism which sees all reality as a process of signs. There is no need to appeal to anything outside or beyond the motion of signs. In particular, we do not need the hypothesis of an eternal cosmic Lexicographer who has antecedently fixed all the basic meanings in a heavenly Book of Words, in order to account for the origin and the first successful use of language. Like Topsy, language 'just growed'. There was no need for anyone to lay down in advance all the right tracks for it to run along.

The Revelation of Being

8. The Contingency of Being, Man and Language

1. For Buddhism as a philosophy and a social doctrine, and the early development of the Ashokan Buddhist State, see Trevor Ling, *The Buddha*, London: Temple Smith 1973.

In the case of Christianity, the conventional separation in the West between Faculties of Classics and Theology, keen to maintain their distance from each other, has always tended to obscure the extent to which, in the late-classical Mediterranean world, both Judaism and Christianity were propagated – and received – as philosophies. A Jewish apologist could confidently compare Moses with Plato to the latter's disadvantage; and Christian art from the mid-third century commonly portrayed Christ as a philosopher-teacher, bearded and robed, seated and reading from a scroll. The later standard iconography descended from this image.

The subject of early Christianity as one philosophy amongst others in the Roman Empire has been opened up by a number of writers, including C.B. Cochrane, E.R. Dodds and H.A. Wolfson. But much more needs to be done.

9. The Temporality of Being, Man and Language

1. In Buddhism this is called 'conditioned co-arising' or 'dependent co-orgination'; (Sanskrit: *pratityasamutpada*, Pali: *paticca-samuppada*). We are thinking of causality in a world without substances, a world in which everything is interwoven and is in a continual flux of passing-away and coming-to-be.

2. A number of the followers of A.N. Whitehead have put forward views of this type. The most notable of them is Charles Hartshorne: see his essay on 'Time, Death and Everlasting Life', in *The Logic of Perfection and Other Essays in Neoclassical Metaphysics*, La Salle, IL: Open Court 1965.

3. For my 'solar ethics', see *After All* (1994), p.109; *The Last Philosophy* (1995), c.15; *Solar Ethics* (1995); and *After God* (1997), pp.89f. Solar ethics is purely expressive living, living (as one might say) unto death, and it is the highest form of affirmation of the world and of life.

10. The Outsidelessness of Being, Man and Language

1. Anselm, *Proslogion* (written at Bec, 1077/8), cc.V–XV.

2. I first aired my 'democratic' and transactionalist notions of meaning and value at a conference in July 1990. See Philippa Berry and Andrew Wernick, edd., *Shadow of Spirit: Postmodernism and Religion*, London: Routledge 1992, c.11, pp.149–155.

11. The Coextensiveness of Being, Man and Language

1. Ludwig Wittgenstein, *Tractatus Logico-Philosophicus*, London: Routledge and Kegan Paul 1922, p.27.

2. I give Loggerheads a capital letter because it is an actual place. Some years ago I received a letter of reference for a clergyman from a man who lives there. He began: 'During the ten years that my wife and I have been at Loggerheads . . .' It took me a long time to discover its exact location, but I felt I had to know. There are, it turns out, *two*; one in England, one in Wales. One is NE of Market Drayton and the other NE of Ruthin.

3. Bernard Williams, *Problems of the Self: Philosophical Papers 1956–1976*, Cambridge: Cambridge University Press 1973, no.6. See p.89.

12. Fear of Being

1. See, especially, Miguel de Unamuno, *The Tragic Sense of Life*, 1913; tr. J.E. Crawford Flitch, New York: Dover Pub., 1921; on Unamuno's relationship to Kierkegaard and Nietzsche, see Susan Serrano, *The Will as Protagonist*, Seville: Padilla Libros, n.d.; and see also Leszek Kolakowski, *Metaphysical Horror*, Oxford: Blackwell 1988.

2. For thoroughgoing postmodernism, see also the recent writings of Mark C. Taylor, such as *Imagologies* (with Esa Saarinen), London and New York: Routledge 1994 and *Hiding*, Chicago: Chicago University Press 1997. The latter book is about the postmodern tendency to bring everything down to 'writing on the skin', and includes a good discussion of the psoriasis of Dennis Potter, the television playwright and author of *The Singing Detective*.

3. Alan Harrington, *The Immortalist: An Approach to the*

Engineering of Man's Divinity, 1969; UK edn., St Albans: Panther 1973.

13. The Love of Being

1. For all this, see *Mysticism After Modernity*, Oxford: Blackwell 1998.
2. Cited from the Temple Classics edition, Dent 1903.
3. See David Hume, *A Treatise of Human Nature*, ed. L.A. Selby-Bigge, Oxford: Clarendon Press 1888 and many later editions; and David Pears, *Hume's System*, Oxford: Oxford University Press 1990.
4. See the discussion in Book I, Part IV, Sect.II of the *Treatise*: 'Of scepticism with regard to the senses'.
5. The *Demiourgos* in Plato's *Timaeus*, sometimes Anglicized as *Demiurge*, is a divine craftsman. He is not an absolute creator, but a craftsman who shapes a given material.

14. The Secular Trinity

1. See *The Religion of Being*, London: SCM Press 1998, p.161.
2. Note that our secular form of trinitarianism has come out Western, teaching the Double Procession.
3. *Mysticism After Modernity*, Oxford: Blackwell 1998.
4. Both published in London by Constable, 1927 and 1929.
5. See Lawrence Stone, *Sculpture in Britain: The Middle Ages*, The Pelican History of Art 9, Harmondsworth: Penguin Books 1955, pp.106, 77f.

Index of Names